Learn How to Study

Learn How to Study

A PROGRAMMED INTRODUCTION TO BETTER STUDY TECHNIQUES

Revised Edition

DEREK ROWNTREE

CHARLES SCRIBNER'S SONS • NEW YORK

Copyright © 1970, 1976, 1983 by Derek Rowntree

Library of Congress Cataloging in Publication Data

Rowntree, Derek.
    Learn how to study.
    Bibliography: p.
    Includes index.
    1. Study, Method of—Programmed instruction.
1.Title.
LB1049.R65   1983   371.3′028′12   82-23187
ISBN 0-684-17881-8 (pbk.)
ISBN 0-684-17971-7

1 3 5 7 9 11 13 15 17 19   F/P   20 18 16 14 12 10 8 6 4 2
1 3 5 7 9 11 13 15 17 19   F/C   20 18 16 14 12 10 8 6 4 2

PRINTED IN THE UNITED STATES OF AMERICA.

For Mark and Leo, should they ever need it

Contents

Preface

Please read this first

This book is written for students of *all* kinds. It will certainly help you if you are a student in a college or university, but it will also be useful to high school seniors and to those taking correspondence courses at home. Whether you are nearing the end of your college years or are just beginning, whether you are confident or anxious, successful or prone to failure, a little time spent thinking about the job of studying will be amply repaid.

The ability to study is not something we are born with (like the ability to breathe)—it is a set of skills that must be learned. Yet few of us have ever considered learning to study: even fewer have been *taught*. But now, year by year, an expanding army of students calls out more and more loudly for some kind of *guidance* on how to set about the job of studying effectively. Some colleges and universities are arranging courses on how to study. Several books have been written about study techniques. This "programmed" book is an attempt to introduce you to some basic study techniques rather more quickly than could be done in a college course and rather more effectively than can be done in normal textbook style.

I hope, in the pages that follow, to persuade you to think critically about an approach to study that has been tested and found effective by large numbers of successful students.

Apart from gaining a basic language in which to discuss study problems with your teachers and fellow-students, you should also be enabled to evaluate the various techniques we discuss and adapt them, where appropriate, to your own needs.

These techniques will include the planning and use of study time, making the best use of a textbook, improving reading and note-taking ability, writing papers, learning from discussion, and dealing with examinations. Most of the book is "programmed"—a kind of writing that calls continuously for active participation by the reader. Three of the chapters are in "normal" prose, however, and to these you are expected to apply what you have learned in the rest of the book.

How to Use this Book

1 As I have said, most of the pages that follow are "programmed." That is, they are divided (by lines across the page) into *frames*. Each *frame* is a unit of teaching, and each one calls for you to do something, or answer a question. Then the correct answer will be given to you at the start of the next frame—below the line.

For instance, you may be asked to think of the word (or words) that completes the sense of a sentence in which I have left a blank (or blanks):

And the correct answer (in *italics*) will be found at the beginning of the next _____ below.

---

frame (This is the correct answer for frame 1.)

2 At other times, I will ask you to choose which of *two or more* words best fills the blank in a sentence. For instance:

The correct answer to this kind of question will still appear at the *(top/middle/bottom?)* of the next frame.

---

top

3 Yet again, I will sometimes ask you a *direct* question, and you should decide your answer before going on to the next frame to check. For instance:

Where do you expect to find the answer to *this* question?

At the top of this frame! (Of course, my answer may often be worded differently from yours, and you will have to decide whether or not you are correct.)

4 Sometimes I will ask you a question like the one at the end of this frame—a multiple-choice question with two or more alternative answers. With this kind of question I will either simply give you the correct answer at the top of the next frame as usual *or* I will give each answer a letter (as below) and, according to your choice of answer, you will go on to read one or other of the lettered paragraphs in the following frame.

Why do you think a programmed book keeps asking you questions?

> To try and trip you up.   **A**
> To help you learn.   **B**
> To give you a test.   **C**

(Look in frame 5 below for the lettered paragraph corresponding to *your* answer.)

---

5 Why are you reading this paragraph? It is not lettered A, B, or C, so it does not correspond with any of the answers. If you want to get the best out of a program (or any other reading for that matter) you must watch out for clues that will help you *skip* material you do not need. Otherwise you will waste a lot of your time. Please go back to frame 4 and decide which of the lettered paragraphs you should be reading.

A. *I am glad to say you are mistaken. I certainly shall not be trying to trip you up. All my questions will be perfectly fair. If you think about the information you are given you should be able to answer them correctly nearly every time. But the questions do have a very important purpose. Please go back to frame 5 and work out what it is.*

B. *This is indeed the purpose. If you read to answer questions, the questions will keep you active, aid your concentration,* *draw your attention to the most important ideas, and keep you informed as to how well you are understanding them. In short, the questions will help you learn. Please go on to frame 6.*

C. *Testing is not the real purpose. The questions only test in the sense that they help* you *keep a check on your own progress: nobody else need ever know what results you're getting. No, the questions in a program have a much more crucial function. Please go back to frame 4 and decide what it is.*

---

6 As you will have noticed, if you have glanced at more than one paragraph of the previous frame, an *in*correct answer to this kind of question leads you to further discussion on the point, and you may then be asked to try again.

Since all these questions are intended to help you learn, it is important that you treat them properly:

N.B. Always decide *your* answer *BEFORE* checking the correct answer shown in the following frame.

Please try to avoid the temptation to peek ahead, for if you do you will not learn so well. The best idea is to keep a *sheet of paper* in one hand as you read, and move it down the page uncovering just one new frame at a time. Do not uncover the next frame until you have made your response to the one before it.

Thus, if you were following my advice, you *(should/should not?)* be able to see the correct answer to this question right at this moment.

---

should not (You would have had the answer covered.)

7 So find yourself a sheet of paper or a card, and use it to cover the frame following any one you are working on.
A few more *hints* and suggestions for getting the most out of this book:

1. Read the chapters in the order I have numbered them.
2. Take a break between one chapter and the next.
3. Do not read more than two chapters in any one day.

4. I give the approximate time required for each chapter, and it is wise not to begin on a new chapter unless you have about that amount of time available.
5. If you do have to break off before the end of a chapter, check back through the earlier frames to refresh your memory before continuing from where you left off.
6. For maximum effect, discuss the program ideas with teachers and with other students wherever you have the opportunity.

Learn How to Study

1 Why Learn to Study?
(Study Time: about 25 minutes)

THE PROBLEM

1.1 Why, you might well ask, should you be expected to spend time reading and thinking about study? After all, haven't you spent most of your life studying? This may be so, but are you sure that the *kind* of study you've done so far will produce results now that you are in college?

For instance, here are some statements about study made among a group of students recently:

> "I sit at my desk for hours on end, but very little really gets done."

> "I seem to spend too much time on some subjects, and not enough on others."

> "I find difficulty getting started; I keep putting it off."

> "It's so difficult to know what's worth learning."

> "In lectures I find I'm either making no notes at all, or else I'm writing down every word the lecturer utters."

> "I can't seem to settle down with any one subject for very long."

> "I don't have enough time to fit everything in."

This is just a selection from many such statements. (Perhaps you could even add one or two of your own.)

How many of these students sound *confident* about their ability to study?

None of these students sounds very confident about studying.
(Nor are they very unusual in this.)

Higher Standards

1.2 Why is it that so many students get through high school
without too much bother, only to find themselves in trouble
at college? Partly it is because standards are so much *higher.*
The student who was one of the best in his senior year may
find he is now below average, among fellow-students who are
all as good as or better than he is. So, quite frankly, work
which once would have earned him grades of A − or B +
may now earn him only C − or D +.

To get the same amount of success in college, you'll need to
do *(less/no more/more?)* studying than you did in high school.

---

more

1.3 So higher standards will involve you in more studying than
you are used to. However, it is not just the amount but
also the *kind* of studying that must change. Now why is this?
In high school, everything was organized for you. You no
doubt had:

1. A full schedule;
2. mandatory class lessons;
3. private study periods;
4. specific homework set for you most evenings.

On top of all this, you knew perhaps that your teachers would:

5. carefully watch your progress from day to day;
6. quickly spot and correct any backsliding;
7. even offer well-intended spoon-feeding if there was any
   danger of your failing an examination.

   In short, you didn't have to worry too much about how to
spend your study time, and you knew that your teachers
would make sure you learned.

Would you say this is all true of *college* also?

No, things are definitely not so organized for you in college.

You Are Responsible

1.4 You are now given much more *responsibility* for your learning. You spend far less time in class, and the college schedule is unlikely to suggest when you should be doing your private studying. You can use your out-of-class time productively for work and recreation, or you can fritter it away doing neither very satisfactorily. You are expected to schedule your own activities.

Your professors may give you several weeks to complete a piece of written work, and probably no one checks to see how you are doing until the day comes to hand it in. You will be given a wide range of new reading to do, probably without being told that certain texts must be read by certain dates. How thoroughly you apply yourself to these learning tasks is entirely up to you.

In short, whether or not you succeed in your studies depends chiefly on . . .

> how well you can learn? **A**
> how well your professors can teach? **B**

1.5 A. *Your professors can help create a stimulating environment in which learning can take place—but this is not the same as teaching you. You must develop your own study methods, set your own targets, and be your own guide. Your teachers will back you up, and may even inspire your efforts, but it is your responsibility to learn. Go on to frame 1.6.*

B. *If you really believe this you'd better throw in the towel right away, or else prepare to change your attitude pretty drastically. In higher education the emphasis is quite rightly on the learner learning rather than on the teacher teaching. Please read paragraph A above before going on.*

How Do You Study?

1.6 To help you be realistic about your present approach to study, here is a quick questionnaire. Consider each question carefully and answer it honestly by writing "yes" or "no."

1. Do you make out a schedule for the studying you will do each day?

   2. If so, do you usually keep to it?
   3. Do you usually study in the same place every time?
   4. Do you have difficulty getting down to work at the start of a study session?
   5. Do you get your written work in on time?
   6. Do you try to contribute to class discussions?
   7. If you are having trouble with your work, do you usually discuss the problem with a teacher?
   8. Do you ever try to analyze your work to see just where you may be weak?
   9. Do you usually glance through a chapter, making a preliminary survey before you read it in detail?
   10. Do you frequently skip tables and graphs when they occur in your reading?
   11. When you come across a word in your reading that you do not know, do you usually look it up in the dictionary?
   12. Do you agree that memorizing is the most important factor in studying?
   13. Do you write notes in skeleton form (that is, an outline of key words and phrases rather than continuous prose)?
   14. In lectures, do you usually take notes just as fast as you can write?
   15. Do you keep all your notes for one topic together?
   16. Do you consciously use ideas you learn in one course to help you in some other course?
   17. When you have to memorize something, do you usually try to do it all in one sitting?
   18. Do you find it difficult to express your ideas in writing?
   19. If an examination or test is sprung on you unexpectedly, do you get a low grade?
   20. Do you sit up late studying the night before an exam?

Write your answers before going on to the next frame.

1.7 The questionnaire you have just completed is based on one tried out by large numbers of college students. Successful students more often than unsuccessful students tended to give the answers shown below:

1. *Yes*	5. *Yes*	9. *Yes*	13. *Yes*	17. *No*
2. *Yes*	6. *Yes*	10. *No*	14. *No*	18. *No*
3. *Yes*	7. *Yes*	11. *Yes*	15. *Yes*	19. *No*
4. *No*	8. *Yes*	12. *No*	16. *Yes*	20. *No*

If you look again at the questions, and at these answers, you will perhaps get some idea of the kind of approach that leads to success. If these answers differ much from your own, you may see where you need to reconsider your study habits.

WHAT IS STUDY?

But before we get down to discussing the problems of study and what can be done to minimize them, we'd better try to agree on just what study is. Maybe you've been at it so long you've never stopped to define it. Well, why don't you try now:

What is study?

Write down a definition before you go on to the next frame.

1.8 Unfortunately, I can't tell what *your* definition is. However, you can compare it with the definitions below. Which of these definitions of study would you *most* agree with?

Following a series of lectures and set work.	**A**
Being taught all there is to know about a subject.	**B**
The memorization of difficult subject matter.	**C**
The systematic pursuit of understanding.	**D**
Preparing to pass a tough examination.	**E**
Devoting all one's thoughts and energies to learning.	**F**
I can't agree with any of these definitions.	**G**

1.9 A. *You have taken rather a passive line here. Following a lecture course is often part of study, but* not a necessary part. *If you were determined enough to set your own study goals and work out how to achieve them, you would be following nobody, yet you'd still be studying. How so? Please return to frame 1.8 and consider the other definitions.*

B. *I thought we'd already decided that learning was now your responsibility? Forget about being taught: those days are over. Higher education is largely a do-it-yourself job. (Besides, nobody ever learned "all there is to know" about a subject.) Please go back to frame 1.8 and look for a slightly more realistic definition.*

C. *This is more like the definition of "cramming" than of "study." You are not a sponge, fit only to soak up facts and figures. You are a human being with the ability to think about and understand ideas. We can store all the information we need in books, on film, and in computers: the human role is not to store information but to use it, analytically and constructively. Your study methods should reflect this emphasis. Please go back to frame 1.8 and look for a better definition.*

D. *This definition does seem to be the best of the bunch (though perhaps not as good as yours). It emphasizes the importance of understanding (rather than merely remembering). It indicates the active role of the student—pursuing rather than merely being led along. It brings in the word "systematic"—implying a considered evaluation of the means to reach a specified goal. Please go on to frame 1.10.*

E. *It is a good thing to have firm targets, but your study should be doing more for you than simply enabling you to pass a particular examination. Exam-centered "study" can too easily lapse into cramming. It is not enough merely to swallow information that can later be thrown up in the examination room. Your studying should involve you in thinking about and understanding your subject, and exam success will be just one byproduct of these activities. Please return to frame 1.8, and look for a better definition.*

F. *Well, at least you've emphasized thinking and the use of energy, but I have the feeling you are overdoing things. It would be a very obsessive, impoverishing kind of study if it left you no thought or energy for other human activities—entertainment and recreation, for example. Please return to frame 1.8 and consider some less total definition.*

G. *Well, I'd have thought we had a pretty fair range of opinion here. Perhaps there are two or more that you simply can't decide between. Perhaps your definition is so different that nobody else could have predicted it. I suggest you take the first opportunity to discuss your definition of study with your teachers or fellow-students. You might also usefully skim through all the paragraphs above (comparing each one with the answer to which it relates), before you go on to frame 1.10.*

1.10 *Study* involves you in deciding goals and choosing methods, solving problems, setting up tests or experiments, collecting information, separating facts from opinions, comparing facts and weighing opinions, and looking for proof and truth.

It demands that you analyze and criticize not only your own ideas but also those of other people, whether you hear them in lectures or discussion, or read them in books and articles.

You will have to make concise notes and summaries to help you remember and to clarify your thinking, and you will have to express yourself clearly and to the point in writing essays, reports, and theses.

In fact, you will be applying all your critical powers to the quick and effective handling of information as you make your way toward definite goals.

If, for the sake of argument, you accept the above definition of study, for *how long* would you expect to be studying?

Well, I asked your opinion. Mine is that studying, in the sense I have described, is something you'll be doing for the rest of your life. (Presumably you will always be collecting and evaluating new ideas, relating them to what you already know, and perhaps explaining them to other people.)

STUDY AS A JOB

1.11 Study is partly a mental attitude, but it is also a *job* which, like any other, has its own skills and work habits which have to be learned. Of course, it takes time and trouble to learn the most efficient ways of doing any job, and it might seem easier just to muddle along. But, once learned, good work habits save untold amounts of time (your time) in the future.

Quite frankly, study will always be hard work. But efficient study techniques will make the hard work . . .

harder?	**A**
easier?	**B**
disappear?	**C**
productive?	**D**

1.12 A. *Only in the sense that it is harder,* at first, *to learn the crawl or breast stroke when all you're used to is the dog-paddle. But when you've learned the more efficient method you can get along a lot faster. Similarly with the techniques of study. Return to frame 1.11 and rethink your answer.*

B. *Perhaps to some extent you are right. Efficient study techniques will allow you to produce better results in a shorter time, and you may well feel under less strain than previously. However, I believe you will still feel you are working hard, but with the encouragement of knowing you are achieving results. Read paragraph D below.*

C. *Never in this life. Study demands critical thinking and this always involves hard work. However, hard work is not always fruitful—it may be misdirected and fail to produce results. The purpose of efficient methods, in study as in any other job, is to make sure that your hard work is not wasted. You may have to work just as hard, but you'll have the encouragement of knowing that you are getting results. Please return to frame 1.11 and choose a better answer.*

D. *Efficient techniques will make the hard work more productive. That is, for a given amount of work done, you'll get more accomplished. The quantity and quality of your results will improve. You will get more done in a given time. Instead of working hard yet still feeling the job is getting on top of you, you'll work hard and have the satisfaction of knowing you are achieving results. Please go on to frame 1.13.*

The Importance of Motivation

1.13 There is one snag we must face. Not all students are really prepared to put in the thought and practice needed to learn new habits. Some believe they can get by as they are. Such students are simply not *motivated* to learn.

Lack of motivation is obviously a deadly enemy of effective study. It results in apathy, boredom, and a general desire to put everything off until another day. Unmotivated students are devoid of drive and imagination, and the spirit of inquiry is usually dead in them. They only do (usually grudgingly) what they are *told* to do. They cannot concentrate. They have difficulty remembering what they have studied.

Do you know any students who fit this description? Do you have any idea *why* they lack motivation?

Almost certainly you'll know some students who use little energy or imagination in the job of studying. It is not always easy to say why, however.

1.14 One reason for a particular student's poor motivation may be the fact that he is no longer being urged along by high school teachers and just doesn't know how to cope now he must think and plan for himself.

Another reason might be *lack of purpose:* this student perhaps has no goals or objectives to aim for. Before you go on to the next frame, stop a moment and honestly answer this question in your own mind:

Why did you go to college?

1.15 *There are many possible answers, and only you know what yours is.*

Here are some of the possibilities:

1. To please my parents/teachers/friends/relatives, etc.
2. Because I did well in high school.
3. The social life attracted me.
4. Because I wanted to train as a teacher/plumber/doctor/ engineer, etc.
5. I couldn't think of anything else to do.
6. To get some further education.
7. To pursue an interest in my major subject.

Clearly, these reasons for attending college are not all equally likely to help a student take the job of studying seriously.

1. Which reason is *least* likely to aid a student's motivation?
2. Which is *most* likely to motivate him?

---

1. *Probably 5 closely followed by 3.*
2. *Almost certainly 4 or 7—with 6 as a (rather vague) runner-up.*

1.16 Whatever the merits of other possible reasons for being in college, the student who is pursuing a *vocational* aim (4) or a strong interest in his *major subject* (7) is the one most likely to develop a professional attitude to the job of studying.

Certainly a *lack* of interest in his or her subject is often the cause of a student's *poor* motivation. What would you recommend a student to do if she was genuinely *un*interested in her *program as a whole?*

The student who has no interest in her program as a whole might well be advised to stop it at once and start looking for something in which she could find satisfaction.

1.17 What more commonly happens, however, is that just *some* aspects of a program of study are less interesting than others. This is something we must learn to live with. It is up to the student to *put interest into* the dull areas, or they will damage her performance in the course.

What would be the best way of handling these uninteresting parts of a program?

a. Forget about them, or
b. Put them off until later, or
c. Work at them.

---

c. *Work at them.*

1.18 Be *extra* active in the subject that least appeals to you. Try to find out why it is important. Talk it over with teachers and students who *are* interested: what makes it attractive to them? (Other people's enthusiasm can sometimes be infectious.)

Approach the subject from a variety of viewpoints. Don't restrict yourself to one teacher or one textbook: find out how different teachers tackle it; ransack the library for the books that will bring the subject home to you.

Above all, try to relate the uninteresting subject to something that you *do* find interesting. (In teaching, one must do this for other people; in learning, one must do it for oneself.) Remember that learning is basically *association,* and the more interests and knowledge you have, the more things you will have to associate new ideas *with.*

Thus, the more you have already learned, the *(harder/easier?)* it will be to learn new things.

---

easier

1.19 New ideas only seem "difficult" or uninteresting when you have no hooks (background) to hang them on. Making these hooks (building up your background in a subject) may seem arduous at first, but the going will become easier and easier—and more enjoyable. There is nothing more motivating than seeing that you have already made progress.

So, we can't always rely on interest to act as the *stimulus:* in some cases we must expect it as the *fruit* of study. If a vital topic is not already interesting, it is up to you to make it so—by an effort of *willpower* and *determination.*

N.B. Before you go on to the next frame, pause a moment to write a rough list of the *main points* you *remember* being made in this chapter.

REVIEW QUESTIONS

These next six frames contain questions that will help you check your memory of the main points of this chapter. If you find any question too difficult, you can get help by looking back to the frames mentioned in brackets after the question.

1.20 What are the two main differences between high school and college learning that may call for improvements in the way you study? (Frames 1–5)

You'll face higher standards and you'll need to take more responsibility for your own learning.

1.21 How would *you* define study? (Frames 6–10)

Whatever your definition, I hope it implies an active *role for the student, a* systematic *approach, and the importance of* understanding *(rather than memorizing).*

1.22 When do you expect to give up studying, in the sense you've defined it? (Frames 10–11)

Never, I hope!

1.23 As a result of learning the techniques of study will you expect to . . .
   a. study every subject in exactly the same way?
   b. spend more time studying?
   c. get more achieved in a given time?
   d. learn everything without effort? (Frames 11–12)

---

   c. *get more achieved in a given time.*

1.24 Which *two* of the following students would be *best* motivated to learn effective study techniques?
   1. A man with a good school record whose chief aim in coming to college is to become captain of both the football and the baseball team.
   2. A woman who has always been interested in archaeology and who wants to do research after majoring in the subject as an undergraduate.
   3. The export sales-manager being paid by his firm to learn French and German who knows that his career prospects depend on the grade he achieves.
   4. The middle-aged man who feels he has missed out in life but that all will be put right if he can get into college to take some courses. (Frames 14–16)

---

   2 and 3

1.25 What should a student do if she finds her program lacks interest? (Frames 17–19)

If only a few parts of her program are uninteresting, she should look for ways of putting interest into them: (talk to other teachers, read other books, relate it to what she is interested in, and so on). If nearly everything in the curriculum is uninteresting, she should seriously consider giving it up.

1.26 Go on to chapter 2 when you are ready.

2 How to Organize Your Studying
(Study Time: about 35 minutes)

Why Bother?

2.1 If you are anything like the majority of students, you'll have suffered from one or more of the following study problems:

1. You feel you simply aren't getting enough done.
2. You do all your work in exhausting fits and starts.
3. You take a long time getting started on a study session.
4. You waste time flitting from one study task to another.

There is only one way to solve, or (better still) avoid these soul-destroying problems, and that way lies through *planning* and *organization*. You must *plan;* how much time you need devote to study; which subjects you will study when; what you intend to achieve during each study session. You must *organize* things so that these goals can be reached.

With effective planning you may even get *more* work done in *(a smaller/the same/a greater?)* amount of time.

---

a smaller (You are *certain* to get more done in the same amount.)

HOW MUCH STUDY TIME?

2.2 The first step in organizing your time is to work out how much time you've got to organize. Obviously, there are

$7 \times 24 = 168$ hours in a week, but they won't all be available for study. Every day you will spend perhaps a *third* of your time asleep, and maybe another couple of hours eating and doing necessary chores. Most days also you will have to do some commuting and attend some lectures and classes (or go to work, if you are not a full-time student). Only you can do the arithmetic and work out how much time will remain for you out of *your* 168-hour week.

It is up to you to decide how this remaining time should be divided between _____ and recreation.

---

study

2.3 Recreation and leisure activities (sports, dancing, conversation, clubs and societies, cinema and theater visits, etc.) are vital to your continued well-being and you should never let them get squeezed out of your schedule. Fortunately, the more you plan your work, the more time you'll find free for relaxation. Each *week* allow yourself:

1. At least *one* regular day off (completely free).
2. Perhaps one morning, one afternoon, and one evening free (preferably from different days).

Even when you have added together eating, sleeping, commuting, classes, and regular times off, you'll find you still have a fair bit of time at your disposal. Take the case of Bill Smithers who has the following weekly time-loads:

sleep	56	hours
eating, etc.	21	
travel	12	(Probably more
classes	24	than *you* spend?)
regular recreation		
(2 working days)	20	
TOTAL	133	hours

Out of the week's 168 hours, this student still theoretically has _____ hours left that he *could* spend on study.

---

35 hours (And this student probably spends more than most on eating, commuting, and attending classes. If you work out your *own* times you'll probably find, unless you work and are a part-time student, that you have quite a bit *more* than 35 hours to spare.)

2.4 But let's face it, few students ever do spend 35 hours a week on private study—except perhaps in the final delirium of exam preparation.

So how much time should be spent on study? I suggest you begin by planning yourself a *weekly minimum of 40 hours' work*—to include lectures, seminars, labs, and all the other scheduled sessions that you are expected to attend, *and* your own private study.

Thus, our Bill Smithers with his 24 hours of classes should spend at least _____ hours on private study.

---

16 hours (This gives him a weekly minimum total of *40* hours' work.)

2.5 Notice that I have put the stress on *minimum*. You should, with practice, be able to work for considerably more than 40 hours a week. But it doesn't do to start off with an over-ambitious plan that you can't possibly stick to at first.

It's far better to start with a modest time-target and learn good work habits: then, once you've got into the routine of doing regular successful studying, you'll find you can add on the odd hour here and there without any agony whatsoever.

During which part of the school year are you most likely to need to do *well over* 40 hours' work a week?

Well, you'll probably need to pile on the effort during any week with an examination or laboratory or fieldwork in it; and by the end of the semester you may well want to clock up 50 hours or more per week.

MAKING A SCHEDULE

2.6 Don't just say "All right then, I'll do 40 hours a week," and simply hope for the best. To make sure of reaching your quota you'll need to work out a schedule.
First consider:

1. Exactly how many hours available for private study? 40 *minus* lecture hours = (probably between 15 and 30 hours).
2. How should these hours be *spaced out* over the week?
3. At what *times of day* should they be used?
4. How should they be divided among your *subjects*?
5. What is the *minimum length* of time for a useful study session?

Let's answer that last question first. What is the smallest usable study session? I suggest you take as your basic study unit the *length of a normal college class period:* that way you'll be able to take best possible advantage of gaps of time between your classes.

So I am suggesting you plan your study sessions in blocks of at least _____ minutes.

---

45 to 90 minutes perhaps?

2.7 Are you thinking "But I can't get anything done in 45 minutes!"? That may be because you normally have to spend 10 of them deciding what to spend the rest on. Once you get into the habit of planning what you want to achieve *before* the time for study arrives, you'll soon find you can make productive use of quite short stretches of time.
So, you have perhaps 18 hours of study to do, and you are going to look in your schedule for gaps of 45 minutes or more. To meet your quota you'll have to allocate a number of these gaps to study. Thus you will arrange with yourself to do 45 minutes on Monday mornings, 2 hours on Monday evenings, 1½ hours on Tuesday afternoons, and so on.
However, we can take this further:

Which of these two possible plans would be most likely to

help you make productive use of Monday morning's study time?

a. You decide to spend 45 minutes on private study, or
b. You decide to spend 45 minutes studying Math.

---

b. *You decide to spend 45 minutes studying Math.*

What to Study

2.8 Planning how to spend your study time is a sure way of helping yourself make productive use of it. Always allocate your study times to *particular subjects*—not just to "study."

Now how do you *share* your time among your various subjects? Clearly, some subjects will need more time because they are more important, say the ones in your major field, or because they demand a lot of reading or writing up.

Again, you may decide your priorities according to how easy you are finding the different aspects of your program. Try making a list of your subjects with the ones you find *most difficult at the top* and the ones you have least trouble with at the bottom. Assuming all your subjects are of equal importance, those at the *(top/bottom?)* of your list should have a larger share of your private study time.

---

top

2.9 Generally speaking, it is wise to spend more time on the most difficult subjects. Review your list every couple of weeks though, because, as you go through the semester, the areas of difficulty will probably shift about from one subject to another.

When to Study

So you should be able to share out your study time among the subjects on your list. Now whereabouts in the week's schedule will you allot time for your study sessions? A good general rule is to do at least some of your studying for

each subject *as close as possible to the class period* for that
subject. (Same day if possible.)
   But *before* or *after* the class period? This depends on the
form that class period usually takes:

When would be the most useful time for a *study session* if the
class period is to be . . .
   1. a straightforward informational lecture? (Before or after?)
   2. a seminar or discussion? (Before or after?)

---

   1. *after* (the informational lecture)
   2. *before* (the seminar discussion)

2.10 A study session right *after a lecture* can be used to review
your notes, check that you really understood what was said,
and follow up any references given. A study session just
before a seminar/discussion gives you the chance to read up
on the background that will help you make an effective
contribution in class.
   One other factor affecting your choice of days for a particular subject is your own *temperament.* It may be, for
example, that you find Tuesdays are best for tackling something new or especially difficult, while on Fridays you are too
tired to do anything but background reading.

What should you do about these differences of mood when
planning your study schedule?
   a. Try to overcome them, or
   b. Take them into account, or
   c. Ignore them.

---

   b. *Take them into account.* (Assign your toughest subjects to
      the days you normally feel at your best.)

2.11 The next question is:
   Which part of the day will you devote to which subjects? Partly
again this will depend on the difficulty of the subject, and on
the sort of work it involves you in.

Your toughest subjects (with the emphasis perhaps on unraveling a complex technical argument, rather than on soaking yourself in narrative-type background) are best studied . . .

   a. in the morning? or
   b. after lunch? or
   c. last thing at night?

---

   a. *in the morning.* (When you are probably at your freshest?)

2.12 Partly, it must be admitted, the timing of a study session within the day must also depend on temperament. Many students are captivated by the glamour of midnight oil, and get a particular kick out of working when everyone else is asleep. But this glamour can seem a bit overrated when you stagger bleary-eyed into a 9:00 lecture the following morning. There's a lot to be said for training yourself to complete your work by midnight.

You should now be able to fill out your *schedule* to cater for:

1. Regular classes, etc. (already scheduled for you).
2. Study sessions, each of at least _____ minutes and each devoted to a particular _____ (and some of them placed _____ to the class period).
3. A total work time (1 and 2 together) of at least _____ hours per week.
4. At least one complete _____ per week booked firmly for regular recreation.
5. Time that can be used for recreation or for additional _____ when the need arises.

---

   2. *45; subject; close*   3. *40*   4. *day*   5. *study*

A Sample Schedule

2.13 As an illustration, let's look at the schedule (page 22) drawn up by Joe Grice—a first-year student in a teachers' college. Joe has about 19 hours of classes per week so, to make up 40 hours of work, he has scheduled another 21 hours for his private study. He decides to spread this time among his eight subjects as follows:

Subject	Study Time	Comment
Geography	6½	Major subject. Maximum time allocation.
Education	5¾	Actually finds this course more demanding than major subject but is counting on getting extra time free for study within the day that is entirely scheduled for Education.
Drama	2¾	Joe's minor subject. He starts off giving it a modest allocation of time, but thinks he may have to increase this later.
English	1	With four of these courses (all on how to
PE	1	teach a subject in grade school) Joe
Art	1	feels he needs spend very little time to
Music	1	keep on top of things. But Math has always
Math	2	been his weak spot and he resolves to give it a little extra time.

total: 21 hours

In case any of these estimates proves insufficient (and realizing that a session set aside for study will sometimes have to be used for some other purpose) Joe has allowed 6 hours (Thursday evening and Friday afternoon) which he could use to catch up on any outstanding work by extra study. Otherwise, he will use these times for extra recreation.

Would you think this is *more* or *less* study than most students of your acquaintance actually do?

2.14 Joe's schedule probably calls for *more* study than most students actually do. However, notice this:

1. Only once does he start before 9:30 in the morning.
2. He finishes work by 9:00 each evening.
3. He has leisurely breaks for meals during the day.
4. He is free all Sunday, most of Saturday, and on one afternoon and one evening during the week.

In short, he has more spare time than most professional or business people, and more indeed than he himself will have when once started on his own career!

N.B. Regular class periods are named in TYPE. Private study sessions are *handwritten*.

Check where Joe has placed his private study sessions in relation to his class periods:

One of his two Geography classes (Wednesday and Friday) takes the form of a lecture, the other a discussion. Can you tell which might be which?

If Joe followed our suggestion from frame 2.10, Wednesday's *will be the* discussion *class, because he scheduled a study session just* before *it;* Friday's *class, with a study session that evening, is likely to be the* lecture.

	Monday	Tuesday	Wednesday	Thursday	Friday	Saturday	Sunday
9:00							
10:00	MATH	*Ed*	DRAMA	ENGLISH	GEOG	*F*	
11:00		COFFEE				*R*	
12:00	MUSIC	ED	DRAMA	*Ed*	GEOG	*E*	
	Math					*E*	*F*
1:00							
2:00			LUNCH				*R*
3:00	*Drama*	ED	*geog*	P E	*FREE*	*geog*	
4:00				SNACK	*or*		*E*
5:00	ART	ED	GEOG	*English*	*CATCH UP*	*geog*	
				PE			*E*
6:00							*E*
7:00					DINNER		
8:00	*Art*	*Ed*	*Drama*	*FREE or CATCH UP*	*geog*	*FREE*	
9:00	*Music*	*Math*	*FREE*		*Ed*		

USING YOUR SCHEDULE

2.15 So, at the very first opportunity (like sometime today) plan out your own study schedule, taking care to label every space. (If you need advice on it, have a word with your adviser or a teacher.)

Where would you think it best to *keep* your schedule once you completed it?

  a. On the wall next to your bed where you'll see it every morning, or
  b. In a notebook which you carry around with you, or
  c. Within sight from the place where you do your studying.

---

  b. *In a notebook which you carry around with you.* (You must be able to refer to it at any time.)

A Daily Work List

2.16 Every morning you will look at your study schedule to check which subjects you have planned to study at which times. Then take it further. Ask yourself *what particular work* you are going to do in each subject. The more precise you are, the surer you'll be of getting results from your labors.

Make a list (preferably on paper) of all the *things to be done* that day. For instance, Joe Grice might have made out his list for one *Thursday* like this:

Check references and plan essay on "streaming."
Listen to tapes of children's poetry and write notes for a follow-up lesson.
Check physiology notes; revise where necessary.
Work through mapwork exercises to prepare for extra seminar tomorrow.

Refer to your list (as well as your schedule) at intervals during the day.

If, at the end of the day, you find you have *not* accomplished all the things on your list, what might you decide to do about them?

Well, it's your decision, and it would depend on how urgent the things were. One solution might be to add them on to your list for the following day.

2.17 Anyway, the main point is that planning a study schedule for a *week* at a time helps you to see what your goals should be for each *day*.

However, your first schedule is not fixed and unalterable for all time. Give it a week's trial run and then ask yourself how successful it has been. Did you manage to keep to it? Did you study the intended subjects at the intended times? Did you get everything done?

If the answer to any of these questions is "No," what might you *do* about your basic schedule before starting the next week?

Surely you would alter your schedule in the light of any difficulties you had experienced with it. (You might need to rearrange your study sessions, allocate your study time differently, or even put in more *study time.)*

REVISING YOUR SCHEDULE

2.18 Remember that your original schedule is simply a useful basis from which to work: you will need to take a critical look at it quite frequently to see whether any temporary or permanent changes are needed. For instance you may need to:

1. Spend more time on a new project or special assignment, or
2. Alter your share of time among subjects because of changes in their relative difficulty, or
3. Make up for study time which you lost, for one reason or another, in the previous week.

How often would you inspect your schedule with this intention of revising it if necessary?

At the beginning of every week *if you are wise.*

2.19 Think well ahead when you are checking your schedule for the coming week. If you know the subject of a paper to be handed in six weeks from now, the time to start planning and reading for it is now. Similarly, if you have tests or exams coming up, don't leave revision until the last moment. Revision sessions are more useful when *spaced-out* rather than when all lumped together. Try to think of each week's work in relation to the whole semester, the whole year, and your whole college career.

What is your reaction to these suggestions about planning your study activities for the week ahead?

I don't believe it would work.	**A**
I think it might be worth trying.	**B**
I haven't got the right kind of personality.	**C**
I think it would take up too much time.	**D**

2.20 **A.** *The evidence proves otherwise. Students who plan their work always have the edge over those who merely drift from one study task to another. The planners have a stronger sense of purpose and priorities, and they get more done in the available time. You may object to planning on other grounds, but not on the grounds that it doesn't work. It does! Please return to frame 2.19 and re-think your answer.*

B. *This seems to me to be the right attitude. Many thousands of students have learned to plan their work and they have almost always reported how their performance has improved. They have a stronger sense of purpose and priorities, and they get more done in the time available. In the early stages, of course, you may have some difficulty in forcing yourself to plan, but stick to it; once you get the knack you'll wonder how you ever let yourself waste so much time in the past. Please go on to frame 2.21.*

C. *If you haven't, nobody has. Let's face it, planning is the way to get a job done as quickly as possible with the minimum amount of fuss. Don't tell me you really want to wander around, not knowing what you are going to be doing from one moment to the next, and probably spending twice as long as you need on every study task?*
   The fact is that many hundreds of students whose first reaction was the same as yours have been amazed to find

*how much their performance has improved once they've tried
seriously to plan their work for a trial period. For all you
know, it may even be your kind of personality that profits
most. Please think about it, anyway, and read paragraph
B above.*

D. *Certainly you may have to spend a whole evening working
out your first schedule. A good deal of thought needs to go
into it. But, thereafter, a few minutes a week is probably
all you need to keep it up to date. The point is, this amount
of time will be repaid over and over again in the increased
productivity brought about by having a schedule that reminds
you exactly what you have planned to do with each unit of
time. Please read paragraph B above before you continue.*

ORGANIZING YOUR STUDY SESSIONS

2.21 So, with a well-planned study schedule, you should be able
to start each day with a list of *things to be done* in your study
sessions.

But some students say "Even when I know what I'm supposed to study, I still don't get very much done in the time."
Such a student's typical "study" evening may well go something like this:

Finishes eating (and chatting) about 7:30 p.m. (had intended to finish at 7:00). Sits down at desk but spends first 15
minutes jumping up and down to collect papers and books,
sharpen pencils, wind clock, etc. Begins to write. Finds
fountain pen needs filling. Goes to borrow ink from friend in
another room. Finds friend with group of students discussing
a new rock group. Stays to state point of view. Some time
passes before remembers is supposed to be studying. Reluc-
tantly goes back to room. Works solidly for next 20 minutes.
Remembers a new record he has bought. Thinks surely can
play it as background music. Attention now shared between
record player and reading. Begins thinking about next
weekend. Goes out to telephone girlfriend. Returns to discover it is nearly 10:00 p.m. and still nothing much done.
Next 40 minutes spent frantically (but hopelessly) trying to
make up for lost time. Following day tells friends he "spent
the whole evening studying." And he believes it himself,
because he only remembers how exhausting it all was.

Does this ever happen to you?

Your answer must surely be "Yes," because, to a greater or lesser extent, it has happened to all of us.

2.22 This frittering away of time is the biggest obstacle to effective study, and the only known cure lies in *planning* and *determination.* Plan exactly what results you want to achieve; be determined about achieving them.

What Are You Going to Study?

In making up your daily list of jobs to be done, be *as specific as possible* about what you plan to do in each study session. (See frame 2.16.) The more precise you are, the more incentive you have to get on with it. Think always in terms of what you want to get done rather than merely of how much time you are going to put in.

For instance, below you'll see three possible items a student might put on his list of jobs to be done. Which of them would give him the best incentive to make effective use of his time?

  a. Spend one hour on *Statistics for the Social Sciences,* or
  b. Spend one hour on chapter 5 of *Statistics for the Social Sciences,* or
  c. Read and make a summary of chapter 5 of *Statistics for the Social Sciences.*

---

  c. *Read and make a summary of chapter 5 of* Statistics for the Social Sciences. (The more specific your goal, the more likely you are to work with concentration and get the job done in the shortest reasonable time.)

Where to Study

2.23 Ideally, you should be able to study anywhere—in a quiet library or on a crowded bus. But let's be realistic. Most of us can't entirely shut off our minds to distractions. So you need to study in a place that is as free as possible from new things and new people that might steal away your attention.
      Also, you need a place that is firmly associated in your mind with serious study. Thus you can slip into the right *frame of mind* the moment you sit down.

So, would you think you'd study best in . . .

a *different* place every day?   **A**
the *same* place every day?   **B**

2.24 **A.** *In one sense you might find it refreshing to go to a different place each day. But only because there would be so many new sights, sounds, smells, and sensations each day that they would quite take your mind off work! (This wouldn't really help you.) Besides, you'd be losing the chance to build up an association between a particular place and work; such an association can be a very useful psychological aid. Please read paragraph B below.*

B. *Familiar places (like your own bedroom or a favorite corner of the library) are likely to hold fewer distractions than new places. And, by constant association of work with a particular place, you can build up the* habit *of getting down to work when you arrive at that place. Please go on to frame 2.25.*

2.25 As for conditions of study, make sure your study place is well-lit and properly ventilated, and neither too hot nor too cold. (Admittedly, it can be difficult to get everything to your liking if you are living in someone else's house or in a dormitory.) The *less* you are aware of your surroundings while studying, the better.

But do remember study is a job. Which of these students is most likely to do the job effectively?

(a)   (b)   (c)

---

b. *(at a table)*

2.26 The best position for study is to sit upright at a table or desk. Bed may be attractive but, once you lie down, sleep is likely to ensue. Even an easy chair may prevent you from doing real study.

So, try to stick to a regular study place. Get plenty of light, don't let the air get stuffy, or too warm or cold, and don't make yourself too comfortable. *Stay alert.*

Having decided your goal for the study session and sat down in your study place, what should you do next?

a. Wait for the urge to work, or
b. Start work right away, or
c. Go through some sort of warm-up procedure.

---

b. *Start work right away.*

Getting Started

2.27 Effective study is largely a matter of good work habits, and starting work right away is one of the very best. Don't wait until you are in the mood, or you may have to wait forever. Don't think that you have to "warm up" in some very individual fashion. Warm up and get into the mood by starting to work. Don't just sit, *do* something.

For example, you might begin by reviewing your lecture notes on the topic you are dealing with. Or you might try to write down the main points you remember from the last piece of work you did on the subject. In fact, it is usually a good opening gambit to spend the *first 5 minutes* of any study session *reviewing* what you last did on that subject. And preferably *write* something down.

Having got yourself started by _____ing what you did last time, the problem then becomes one of how to _____ *(What would be your problem?).*

---

review
concentrate (How to do this will be most people's problem.)

Concentration

2.28 You can train yourself to concentrate and keep paying attention, but it takes will power and persistence. These hints may help you:

1. If you find it difficult to concentrate on a particular subject, start off by studying it in *very short bursts* only. Don't give up a whole evening only to accomplish nothing. Put all you've got into 45 minutes at a time. If even this is a terrible prospect, cut it right down to say, 20 minutes, but have something very *definite* to do. You must prove to yourself that you can keep hard at it, even if only for a very short spell. Gradually, you'll be able to build up to a basic *minimum* of 45 minutes.
2. If you find yourself daydreaming, or drifting away from your goal, *stop it* immediately. Unless you are clearly in need of a definite break, force your attention back to the job you are trying to get done.
3. In every hour of study you will perhaps need a *break* of between 5 and 10 minutes (or two shorter breaks). Stand up, walk around, turn your mind to something else. But take a clear break and then get right back to the job at hand.

So, if you find it difficult to concentrate, practice over very _____ periods of study time, _____ daydreaming the moment it starts, and count on taking breaks totaling up to _____ minutes in every study hour.

---

short   stop   10

2.29 Another aid to concentration is to *make notes*. Try to make some sort of record of what you have achieved in the time you've spent on study. Apart from keeping you active and alert, these records will help you review later.

Ending a Session

Try not to finish a study session at a tough spot in the subject. This will make you less than eager to return to it next time. Aim to leave off at a *point of interest*—one where it will be reasonably pleasant to pick the subject up again.

Use the last 5 minutes of your study session to *recall* what you have studied and to check through it once more. (This is often the *most vital part* of study, and we'll be discussing it further in the next chapter.)

So, a study session of one hour might begin with _____ minutes spent reviewing the previous work, have between _____ and _____ minutes' break somewhere in the middle, and wind up with about _____ minutes' review of the session's work.

---

5   5   10   5

2.30 So you should now be able to plan a study schedule, find a suitable place to work, and decide exactly what results you want from each study session and how to achieve them.

N.B. Before going any further, pause a moment to *note* the main points you *remember* from this chapter.

Then go on to frame 2.31.

REVIEW QUESTIONS

The questions in the following frames should help refresh your memory. If you are unsure of an answer you can look back to the frames mentioned after the question.

2.31 How many hours have I suggested you spend on study (private sessions plus classes) in a normal week? (Frames 4–5)

---

40 at least

2.32 To make sure of reaching your quota of study hours and getting good value from them, you should plan out a study _____ for the week ahead. (Frames 6–14)

---

schedule

2.33 What do *you* regard as the minimum length of time for a useful study session? (Frames 6–7)

You should be able to make effective use of an hour or even less, provided you have a plan for the session.

2.34 Each session on your weekly schedule should be allocated not just to "study" but to (*what?*). (Frames 7–8)

---

a particular subject

2.35 For what kind of class period would you plan a study session . . .

    1. just *after?*
    2. just *before?* (Frames 9–10)

---

    1. *lecture*   2. *discussion*

2.36 How often should you look at your schedule once you have produced it?

    a. Never again, or
    b. Once a week, or
    c. Once a day, or
    d. Several times a day. (Frames 15–16)

---

    d. *Several times a day.*

2.37 Every morning you should look at your schedule to check which subjects you will be studying when. To make sure of getting worthwhile results from these study sessions you should then write out a list of (*what?*).
(Frames 16–17)

---

a list of study tasks to be done that day.

2.38 Here is one student's list of jobs to be done. Which of them would you expect him or her to be able to do (a) *most*, and (b) *least* effectively? Why? (Frames 16 and 22–23)

1. Spend the morning on meteorology.
2. Write history essay from draft outline.
3. Revise for exams.

---

a 2.   b 3.

Number 2 is the most clear and specific description of a job to be done; number 3 is the vaguest.

2.39 What is the best way of getting started on a study session? (Frames 26–27)

Begin work right away (perhaps by reviewing what you did last time).

2.40 How can you train yourself to keep concentrating? (There are three ways at least.) (Frames 28–29)

Work for short periods but with a very definite aim. Watch out for daydreaming and stop it at once. Take definite breaks. Take notes. (You may have thought of still other methods.)

2.41 What is a good way to round off your study session? (Frames 29–30)

Try to recall what you have learned, or check through what you have accomplished in the session.

2.42 In the next chapter we'll be discussing a strategy that will help you with a job that must occupy many of your study sessions—how to get information from a textbook or article.

Please go on to chapter 3 when you are ready.

3 How to Tackle a Textbook

(Study Time: about 55 minutes)

3.1 Whatever else you do with your study time, you are bound to spend a lot of it on books and articles, trying to extract, and organize for your own purpose, the ideas they put forward. But you need to be selective in this reading. At the start of a course you may be presented with a reading list as long as your arm, and if you try to plough through everything on it, sentence-by-sentence, you'll find new titles are being added faster than you can cross the old ones off.

Clearly, you just haven't got time to read everything; and each text you do tackle will need to be approached differently according to what you hope to get from it. Remember what Francis Bacon wrote 350 years ago:

> Some books are to be tasted, others to be swallowed and some few to be chewed and digested; that is, some books are to be read only in parts, others to be read but not curiously [i.e. not carefully], and some few to be read wholly and with diligence and attention.

Bacon describes *(how many?)* different ways of approaching a text.

---

three

3.2 Bacon's three approaches to a text (whether book or article) are just as useful today:

  a. *tasting:* referring to isolated passages of the text.
  b. *swallowing:* skimming lightly and rapidly through the whole text.

   c. *chewing and digesting:* studying the whole text carefully
with close attention.

To choose the best way of tackling any particular book,
you need only ask yourself what you hope to get out of it. Do
you wish, for instance, to:

1. Get a broad, overall picture of a subject?
2. Gain a detailed, organized knowledge of all the essential
   facts and ideas of the subject?
3. Check on a reference/answer a specific research question?

Which of Bacon's three approaches (a, b, or c) would you
consider most appropriate for each of these three different
purposes in reading?

I would choose b *for purpose 1,* c *for purpose 2, and* a *for
purpose 3.* Do you agree?

3.3 So, when tackling books and articles, your strategy should
be flexible: you should be ready to skim or to read with close
attention, in full or in parts, according to what you are
looking for. One strategy that has proved very successful and
can be adapted to most kinds of reading is often known as

SQ3R

This stands for the *five* steps in studying a book (or chapter,
or article):

   Survey
   Question
   Read
   Recall
   Review

According to this formula, the student should:

1. Get the general drift of what he is to study by carrying out
   a preliminary _____ of the text.
2. Ask himself _____s that he expects to have answered by
   the time he has finished reading the text.
3. _____ the text.
4. Try to _____ the main points.

5. Go back and _____ the text to check how well he has picked out the main points.

---

1. *survey*   2. *question*   3. *read*   4. *recall*   5. *review*
(Say this over to yourself a few times so as to get the sequence into your head.)

3.4 This SQ₃R approach has helped bring success to thousands of students, and it is worth thinking about in detail. Let's take it step by step:

SURVEY

So many of us, when we study a printed text, will "begin at the beginning, go on until the end, and then stop." This, however, is a useless way to read. We don't know where we are going, and we soon get so bogged down in detail that we can't see the forest for the trees. Instead, we should try to get a bird's-eye view of the forest before we begin trampling through the undergrowth. We should *survey the whole* before we try to understand the parts.

Making a preliminary _____ of a book or article before you begin to read is like planning out your route on a _____ before you begin a difficult journey.

---

survey   map

Surveying a Book

3.5 All books and articles are written to some kind of *plan*. A quick survey can give you a very good idea of what this plan is, and will therefore help you read with better understanding.

Title page. Start your survey with the title page. You may think you won't get much from it, but it's always worth a glance. It can tell you:

1. The general subject area—(the title itself).
2. The level or approach—(subtitle or descriptive phrase).

3. The author's name and qualifications—(degrees, insti-
   tution).
4. The date of publication—(on the back of the page).

How much of this information can you get from the title page
of the book you are looking at *now*? Please turn to the front
matter (if you didn't do so earlier) and take a look.

The title page tells you that this book is about studying, *that it
is merely an* introduction *to study techniques, and (very
important) that it is* programmed. *It also tells you the name
of the* author, *indicates the* experience *out of which the
book has arisen, and tells you (on the reverse side) how*
recent *the book is.*

3.6 So much for your five-second analysis of the title page.
What next?

Preface. Whether it goes by the name of Preface, Foreword,
Author's Remarks, Introduction, or whatever, far too few
people ever read the section at the front—usually just a few
paragraphs—in which the author talks about his book and
why he wrote it. Like the title page, this information can help
you decide whether the book is worth your reading, and
even *how* you might set about it.

Look back at the Preface to *this* book, for example. It
consists of four paragraphs followed by a final "programmed"
section, each giving you a different kind of information.
(For instance, the first paragraph tells you *who* the book is
intended for.)

What kind of information is given by each of the other paragraphs and by the final section of my Preface?

3.7 The four paragraphs and final section of my Preface contain
information on:

1. *Who the book is written for.*
2. *Why it is necessary.*
3. *The scope and purpose of the book.*
4. *The outline and structure of the book.*
5. *How to use the book.*

Contents. This again is a page (or more) of information that you should never ignore when making your preliminary survey. The contents tells you what topics the author is dealing with and very often gives you some idea of how he or she has organized them—main topics, subtopics, and so on.

Look back at the contents for *this* book:

1. Of the following possible topics for a book about study, which are *not* given a chapter of their own?
   essay writing
   note-taking
   studying a textbook
   reading
   discussions
   lectures
   psychology of study
   organizing study time
   choosing courses
   the need to learn study techniques
   examinations
2. In all, there are _____ chapters and each one has between _____ and _____ subsections.

---

1. *The book does* not *contain chapters on lectures, the psychology of study, or choosing courses.*
2. *In all, there are* eight *chapters and each one has between* four *and* seven *subsections.*

3.8 So your survey of a contents page tells you *what* is covered by the book and, if it is subdivided, may give some clue as to *how* the topics are related to one another. Later, as you read through the chapters, you should *return* often to check the contents again.

  .   If your purpose in picking up the book was simply to look up references that might help answer a *specific* question, your preliminary survey might well *end* at this point. You can see from the contents whether or not the book is likely to contain anything useful.

If it is, then you can turn straight to the *back* of the book where you should be able to look up your topic in an alphabetical list telling which topics occur on which pages; this list is called an _____ .

---

index (Does this book have one?)

3.9 If you were simply looking for specific references, the index would save you a lot of time by directing you at once to the most useful passages. As the newspaper columnist, Robert Lynd, once said, "I hate reading a book without an index: it makes me read the whole book."

If, however, you do decide the whole book (or even a complete chapter), is worth "chewing and digesting," take one last step in your general survey:

Leaf through the book. Run fairly quickly through the pages of the book from front to back. While leafing through:

1. Read the chapter and section headings.
2. Read the end-of-chapter summaries (if any).
3. Look at any charts and illustrations.
4. Glance at an occasional sentence.

Needless to say, very little of what you see will stick in your mind at this stage. However, this quick run-through does add to what you have already guessed about the structure of the book and, like all surveying, it gets you *prepared* for the task that is to come.

Take my word for it then. Note where you have got to so far, and then leaf very quickly through the rest of *this* book to get a *general impression* of its contents. (Follow the four suggestions given above.)

Well you should now know where you are going and what sort of journey you are likely to have. (At the very least you should have noticed that three of the chapters are not written in programmed form like those you have read so far.)

3.10 So, I have suggested that when you first approach a book you should start with a general survey.
To do this you must:

1. Read the _____ page.
2. Read the author's remarks, or _____ .
3. Read the table of _____ .
4. Leaf quickly through the entire _____ .
5. How long do you think you might need to spend on this overall survey? Between _____ and _____ minutes.

---

1. *title*
2. *preface (or introduction, etc.)*
3. *contents*
4. *book*
5. *I asked your opinion of how long should be spent on the overall survey. Of course, it must depend on how big the text is and how important it is likely to be to you. My own feeling is that you'll need at least 5 minutes to do a worthwhile survey but probably not more than 30 minutes even if the book is to be the backbone of your course.*

3.11 Very well, you've invested a fair bit of time in surveying the whole book, for you expect to reap the dividends when you actually come to reading it. Do you, therefore, now start to read, sentence by sentence, from the beginning of chapter 1? No, you do not. You need to spend a couple more minutes at the survey stage. In fact:

Now you have completed your general survey of the book as a whole, you should do a more detailed survey of the first _____ .

---

chapter

Surveying a Chapter

3.12 Before you begin *each* new chapter you should survey it— *more carefully* than you did when getting an idea of the book as a whole. Pay special attention to:

First and last paragraphs. The author may use them to give his survey of what is to come, or a summary of what he has said.

Summaries. These may appear at intervals, during the chapter as well as at the end.

Headings. Most authors have gone to considerable trouble to organize their ideas under a helpful system of headings and subheadings. Sad to say, many students completely ignore the headings, and the vital clues contained in them; they try to read a highly structured text as though it were a novel.

Obviously, headings tell you *what* topic is dealt with in each section or subsection. But there's more to them than that. For instance:

What can you tell from the *relative sizes* or prominence of headings? (Look, for example, at the four headings on this frame.)

The relative sizes of the headings tell you how the topics are related to one another—how they go together and which comes under which.

3.13 You must be aware of the *grades* of headings in whatever you are reading. Since they tell you which topics belong with which, they are the key to the author's *structure of ideas.*

Most textbooks will use two or three grades of heading, the type decreasing in size and prominence from chapter heading to section heading to subsection heading and so on. (Thus the *difference* in prominence among the headings on the previous frame told you that it dealt with three aspects of the topic mentioned in the main heading there.)

How many *grades* of headings have I used in this chapter so far? (Note how they show up the relationships between my topics.)

Apart from the main title of the chapter, I have used three grades of heading. Here are the actual headings again, arranged to show the relationship between the topics dealt with in their sections:

3.14 Grade 1   SURVEY

Grade 2 **Surveying a Book**   **Surveying a Chapter**

Grade 3 ***Title page***   ***First and last***
        Preface   ***paragraphs***
        Contents   ***Summaries***
        Leaf through the   ***Headings***
        book

You might like to finish this survey by examining the remaining headings in the chapter.

Once your survey of a chapter is complete, you are ready to move on to the second stage on the SQ₃R method, which is _____ .

Question (The second step of the SQ₃R approach—survey, question, read, recall, review.)

QUESTION

3.15 Never begin the detailed reading of a text without having in mind a set of questions that you want answered. Questions are a great stimulus to learning for they give you a sense of *purpose* and keep you alert. You become an active researcher rather than a passive browser.

     Where do the questions come from? The main source is you:

One of the benefits of making a preliminary _____ of a book or chapter is that it gives you the chance to think up some relevant _____s.

---

survey   question

Your Own Questions

3.16 In surveying the book as a whole, your questions are likely to be pretty general ones. Glancing at the title page, preface, and table of contents, for instance, you might ask yourself:

     "How far can I trust this book, published ten years ago?"
     "Will it be as helpful to *me* as its preface suggests?"
     "Why does the author think it worth giving a whole chapter to such-and-such a topic?"

Even these *general* questions are of some help to you in deciding how to treat the book.

But when you turn from surveying the book as a whole to surveying the chapter you are about to read, your questions will become much *(more/less?)* specific.

---

more

3.17 *Headings* and subheadings of sections should always bring questions into your mind. For instance, when you saw the heading "Question" a couple of frames ago, you might have asked:

"Why has the author used this as a heading? Who questions whom? What part do questions play in study? Where do they come from? How do I find the answers?" and so on.

Some of these questions are already answered, others soon will be.

Look at the next three headings (on frames 3.19, 3.20, and 3.23). What *questions* do they bring to your mind?

"Other people's questions" might lead you to ask: "Which other people? Students? Authors? Teachers? Are their questions as useful as my own? Where do I find the answers?" and so on.

"Questions in programmed learning" might prompt: "What is programmed learning? What do such questions have to do with study? What use are they? What sort of questions?" and so on.

"Read" might suggest: "Don't I know how to do this already? Do I have to learn new ways? What does he say here that is not in the chapter on reading?" and so on.

3.18 So *headings* should be a very fruitful source of questions— questions that give you a sense of purpose. You should be able to take practically any heading and pull at least one question out of it, if only "What does it mean?"

Questions should also come to mind as you look at the *first and last paragraphs,* and at any *summaries.* For example:

"Where are the facts to back up these statements? Can I be mistaken in what I thought I knew about this subject? Have I come across these technical terms before?" and so on.

Are you (as the reader) the *only* source of questions?

No. (As you should remember from your survey of the following heading!)

Other People's Questions

3.19 Sometimes your *teacher* may suggest questions to bear in mind while reading a particular chapter. Or your *fellow-students* may pose questions (or offer comments that are easily re-phrased as questions) about chapters they have had to struggle with.

But perhaps the most useful outside source of questions can be the book itself. The *author* will often pose three or four questions at the beginning of a chapter, and their answers should have become apparent to you by the time you reach the end.

Sometimes authors give you a list of questions at the *end* of a chapter. Since questions are generally more helpful if posed at the *start* of a reading session, you should:

Take note of these end-of-chapter questions during your preliminary _____ of the chapter, and then consider them again after you have finished _____ing it.

---

survey   read

3.20 Unfortunately, students too often take no notice of the author's questions and thereby pass up a very helpful guide to study.

Questions in programmed learning. In a programmed book (like this one) questions play an essential part in the flow of the argument, and you can learn a lot about how to read from the way programs are written.

The author of a program asks questions of many kinds (direct, multiple choice, fill-in-the-blanks), but his or her purpose is always the same—to draw your attention to the

most important point he or she is putting across and make you respond to it.
And your response to the question helps you to _____.

learn (or understand).

3.21 Programs are a fast and effective way of learning and, gradually, more and more material is appearing in this form. There are programs in many school subjects (particularly Math, Science, and English Grammar) and an increasing number at college level.

But programs can teach you something almost more valuable than the subject matter they contain. That is, they can get you into the habit of *reading questioningly*.

In a sense, you should mentally "program" everything you read. Constantly ask yourself questions: "What is the *most crucial idea* in this chapter? This section? This paragraph?" Questions like How? When? Who? Where? and (especially) So what? should rarely be out of your thoughts as you read. And as one question is answered, another should arise.

Normally the answers to your questions will emerge from the text as you read on. What action might you take if an important question is *not* answered in the ensuing text?

Well, if it was an important question you might feel inclined to make a note of it and seek the answer elsewhere—from a teacher, another student, another book, etc.

3.22 So, one of the most important reasons for making a preliminary survey is that you get a chance to raise a few questions that will give purpose to your reading. At first you may find question-raising difficult but, with practice, you will soon do it automatically. If you read questioningly, the questions will come.

Having made your *survey* and started to *question* you are now ready for the third step in the SQ₃R approach which is to _____ the text.

read

READ

3.23 So reading is the third step in studying a book, *not* (as many students appear to think) the first and only step.

Now what kind of reading is called for? Certainly not the kind that most people use with fiction—in an attempt to "take one's mind off things." Your purpose is the very reverse of this: you are trying to *apply* your mind, with all its critical skills.

In fact, as we have just decided, you must read *actively*—in search of *answers*. Remember:

The reader with a _____ to be answered is a reader with a *purpose*.

---

question

Look for the Main Idea

3.24 Perhaps the most purposeful question you can ask yourself is, as I've suggested before, "What is the *main idea?*" Main ideas can be found at each level of the book. The book as a whole will have, perhaps, one very general main idea. The main idea of each chapter will be less general. Each section within a chapter will have a more specific main idea, and the main idea of each paragraph will be most specific of all. Your job is to pick out the main idea *at each level*. Let's try this: Below are four *main ideas* from the book you are reading now:

a. "One effective study technique is the SQ$_3$R approach."
b. "The chief aim in reading should be to find the main ideas."
c. "The reading step in SQ$_3$R must be active and purposeful."
d. "Most students would benefit from more effective study techniques."

Which of these main ideas belongs to:

1. the book as a whole?
2. this chapter of the book?
3. this section (headed "Read")?
4. the paragraph above (starting "Perhaps")?

Write down your answers, then turn to frame 3.25.

---

1. *d*   2. *a*   3. *c*   4. *b*

3.25 *The author's plan.* If you read a book critically, you should be able to detect its hierarchy of ideas—the author's plan whereby the main idea of the *book* (level 1) *breaks down* into a number of more specific main ideas each of which is the theme of a *chapter* (level 2), and each chapter's main idea breaks down to provide main ideas for each of its *sections* (level 3), and each section idea provides even more specific main ideas, one for each paragraph (level 4).

This diagram could illustrate the hierarchy of ideas (each circle representing a main idea) for a small book or pamphlet:

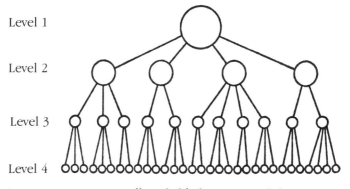

In your *surveys,* you will probably have grasped the main ideas at levels _____ and _____ , and perhaps at level _____ also; at the *read* step of SQ₃R you will be concerned chiefly with the main ideas at level _____ .

---

1   2   3   4
(At the *read* step of SQ₃R you'll need to pick out the main idea from each *paragraph.*)

Two Don'ts

3.26 Do *not* attempt to make notes during the *read* step. To do so can be distracting and it slows you down. Also, it produces the temptation to note the author's words rather than your own, and this is no help at all to understanding and learning. Do *not* underline words or phrases, either—not on *first* reading. Although it might give you a feeling of being active, you'd too often find, on reflection, that you'd underlined the wrong things.

So, on first reading, you should look for the _____ _____s, but should neither _____ portions of the text nor make _____s.

---

main idea   *underline*   *note*

Read It Again

3.27 Many students find it useful to read the text *twice* at this step in SQ₃R. Here is what they would advise.

1. Read straight through the material concentrating on the *main ideas*. Don't stop to underline or take notes. Just put quick check marks in the margin with pencil whenever you see an important idea. (Or, if the book does not belong to you, put slips of paper in the book.)
2. Read through a second time, confirming that you really have picked out the main idea, but this time paying rather more attention than before to the *supporting detail*. Underline the main idea in each paragraph and any important details. (But only, of course, if the book belongs to you.)

So, having done your preliminary _____s and asked yourself _____s, you have _____ the text *twice* and have marked its _____ ideas. You are now ready to take the fourth step in SQ₃R by trying to _____ what you have studied.

---

survey   *question*   *read*   *main*   *recall*

RECALL

3.28 The business of studying a text is not over when you've finished reading even if the material is perfectly straightforward. For instance you have presumably had no difficulty in *understanding* the ideas you've read in this program.

Does this mean you will be able to bring them all back to mind, say a week from now?

Almost certainly not, *unless you are gifted with an exceptional memory. Most people forget 50 percent of what they read within* seconds *of putting down a book—except when they make an* active *attempt to recall.*

The Value of Recall

3.29 Make regular attempts to recall and you'll improve your learning in three ways:

1. You'll *concentrate* better because you'll know you have the task awaiting you.
2. You'll have the chance to *remedy* any lapses of memory or misunderstandings.
3. You'll be kept *active* because you must come to grips with what you have read and summarize it in your own words.

Could you get all these benefits simply by going back and *reading through the text once again*?

No, *a rereading is no substitute for recall. (As you surely know, the fact that you can recognize ideas once you see them again is no proof that you can* remember *them without the book in front of you, let alone put them into your own words.)*

How Often to Recall?

3.30 Once you have started reading, then, you should *pause* frequently and *tell yourself the main points* you have read. Sometimes it will be sufficient to stop at the end of every chapter and recall.

But usually, unless the chapter is very short, you'd be wise to recall *also* at the end of every . . .

> sentence?   **A**
> paragraph?   **B**
> section?   **C**

3.31 **A.** *Unless you were reading extraordinarily long sentences, you would not be wise to try recalling at the end of each one you read. To do so would make your learning too piecemeal, and you would probably lose sight of, or never see, the main ideas. You'll need to take larger bites at the material if you want to get it organized in your mind. Please return to frame 3.30 and reconsider your answer.*

B. *With an exceptionally long or involved paragraph it may sometimes be worth looking away from your book a moment to see if you can summarize that paragraph in your mind. But it would not be wise to get into the habit of stopping after every paragraph (or even couple of paragraphs) since this might prevent you from following the flow of the author's argument. Please read paragraph C below.*

C. *If you waited until the end of a long chapter you might already have forgotten so much that your recall would be far too hazy. But to recall at the end of every sentence or paragraph would make your learning weak and disjointed. The best plan, then, is to go for a section at a time. Every time you see a new* main heading *come up, stop and recall the chapter so far.*

Then recall *again,* covering *all* the sections this time, when you get right to the end of the _____ . Go to frame 3.32.

---

chapter

Make Notes

3.32 Don't just *think* your recall. *Write down* the key points you remember. Make brief *notes* of the main ideas and any details you think important.
Even the sketchiest note-taking is far more valuable than simply allowing half-formed memories to drift through your mind. It is easy to be *overconfident* about how much one remembers—until one tries to pin it down in words. (Besides, you need a *record* of what you have read. More about this in chapter 6.)

So you should start taking notes as part of the _____ step in the SQ₃R approach.

---

recall

How Much Time on Recall?

3.33 Quite a sizable chunk of your SQ₃R time should be spent on the *recall* step. As an example, consider the reasonably well-organized and meaningful material you are likely to meet in courses on education, psychology, economics, or geography: here perhaps 50 percent of your study time should be spent recalling what you have read.

Taking this as a measure, would you expect to have to spend *more* or *less* than 50 percent of your time recalling:

1. Material that has to be learned by heart, e.g., rules, symbols, names, laws, formulae?   _____ than 50 percent.
2. History, philosophy, literature, biography, and any material with a "storylike" content?   _____ than 50 percent.

---

1. *probably* more *than 50 percent (perhaps as much as 90 percent)*
2. *probably* less *than 50 percent (maybe only 20 percent)*

3.34 So be prepared to spend *half* your study time recalling what you have read (and even more if the material is difficult to remember). Experiments have proved that this is not time wasted. In fact, the time-wasters are those people whose aim is simply to "get one more book out of the way." Even if they understand while they read, they will soon forget.

Having made notes of what you recall, you are now ready for the fifth and final step of SQ₃R: you _____ everything you have done so far.

---

review

REVIEW

3.35 Here your purpose is to check the truth of your recall. Never try to convince yourself that you remember everything correctly: always *look again* to make sure.

How to Review

Your best line of action is to do a quick *repeat* of the previous four steps:

1. *Survey* the general structure of the section or chapter. (Look again at the headings and any summaries.)
2. Remind yourself of the *questions* you asked. Can you answer them all? Do any new questions arise?
3. *Reread* the text to see that you've remembered everything of importance.
4. Complete your *recall* by filling any holes and correcting any faults in your notes.

Try this now with the chapter so far:
First *recall* the headings and the main points, making some brief *notes* from memory.

Then follow the four steps of *review* to check how well you have remembered.

How well did you do? Better than you normally expect to, I hope. (But not as well as if you'd tried to recall after *each* of the five sections.)

3.36   The five steps of SQ$_3$R have been tried out by thousands of college students, who have reported very favorably on the increased effectiveness with which they have come to study. Almost certainly you too could benefit from the same approach. You might need to *bend it and adapt it,* or alter the balance or the timing of its steps, to suit your individual needs, but the basic strategy is *flexible* enough for you to use it many different ways and still get good results.

Suppose three different students were to offer the three different views of SQ$_3$R that I describe below. Which view would you think most *practical*?

"It doesn't matter in what order you take the steps as long as you don't miss any out or try to take two steps at once."   **A**

"The steps will overlap to some extent and an early step may even need to be repeated later in the sequence."   **B**

"Each step must be completely finished before the next
one can begin."   **C**

3.37 **A.** *I'm not sure how practical (or even possible) it would
be to recall before you had read, or review before you had
surveyed, so the order of steps in SQ₃R is surely the logical
one. Certainly it would be unwise to leave out any of the
steps, but as for taking two at once. . . . Please read paragraph
B below.*

B. *Although the steps of SQ₃R are in the natural, logical order
and should therefore be followed, we must expect some
overlap and repetition between them. For instance, even while
the emphasis is on survey or read, we may still be asking
questions; or we may want to interrupt the read step in order
to recall and review or to repeat our survey of the text.
SQ₃R gives you a flexible approach that can be varied according to your purpose and the kind of material you are
studying. Please go on to frame 3.38.*

C. *When you come to apply the SQ₃R technique in practice
you will find it difficult to stop asking questions once you
reach the read step, to avoid reading when you come to
review, and so on. Please read paragraph B above before you
continue.*

3.38 There is one final question we ought to consider before
winding up this chapter:

So far we've talked about the SQ₃R approach only in relation
to *texts:* books, reports, articles, etc.
Do you think *any or all* of the five steps could be applied to
the kind of studying you do in a *lecture?*
If so: *Which* steps? *How* would you apply them?

Compare your judgment with mine:

1. *Survey.* Difficult to apply to a lecture unless the lecturer
   herself is prepared to tell you where she is heading. Some
   are, however, and it is always worth asking.

2. *Question.* Preliminary questioning may be difficult without the cooperation of the lecturer, but even so you should be able to think up general questions as soon as you know of the subject, and you should certainly be able to *listen questioningly* once she has begun to speak.
3. *Read.* Impossible unless she provides you with a copy of her notes, but of course *listen* serves exactly the same function.
4. *Recall.* Entirely practicable, and even more *essential* than it is with books.
5. *Review.* Possible in so far as you can check what you recall against what other people thought they heard. And if there are points you still aren't sure about, you can ask the lecturer.

3.39 So, to a large extent, the SQ₃R approach is applicable to lectures as well as books. Try it anyway: it's such a powerful technique that it can adapt itself to give *some* help in almost any type of study (even fieldwork, laboratory work, tutorials, and so on). Certainly you should be able to adapt it to tackle any films, tape recordings, or television programs that form part of your course load.

In the next chapter you have a chance to apply SQ₃R to a real text. But first, check through the following review questions which should remind you of some of the main ideas in this chapter.

REVIEW QUESTIONS

(If any question gives you difficulty, turn back to the appropriate frames.)

3.40 List in order the five steps of SQ₃R. (Frames 3–4)

---

survey   question   read   recall   review

3.41 What steps might you take in surveying a book *as a whole*? (Frames 5–11)

Read the title page, the preface, and the contents (together perhaps with the index); and leaf quickly through the book.

3.42 Before reading an article or a particular chapter within a textbook, it is necessary to survey it in more detail. What are the *three* things you would look at in surveying a chapter? (Frames 12–14)

First and last paragraphs, summaries, and headings.

3.43 At what steps of SQ$_3$R should you be asking questions? (Frames 16–22)

Mainly at the question *step (which tends to mingle with the* survey *and the* read *step), but also during* recall *and* review. *In fact, questions should arise at* all *steps.*

3.44 In tackling a textbook you have to sort out the *main ideas* at all levels from the book, to the chapter, to the section, to the paragraph. At the *read* step you will be chiefly concerned with the main ideas at *which level?* (Frames 25–26)

---

paragraph

3.45 There are *two* things which you should *avoid* doing on *first reading* of a text. *What* are they? *Why* avoid them? (Frame 26)

Do not take notes or underline. (While reading you would be too likely to use the author's words instead of your own, and on first reading you might well underline the wrong things.)

3.46 At what points should you *recall* during your study of a textbook? (Frames 30–31)

At least at the end of every chapter, and most probably at the end of every section within the chapter as well.

3.47 What should you do at the *recall* step? (Frame 32)

Write down the main things you *remember.*

3.48 Why is it necessary to *review*? What should you do at the review step? (Frame 35)

To check the truth of your recall;
Remind yourself of your survey and the questions you asked,
reread the text, and complete your recall by polishing up your
notes.

3.49 The next chapter is unprogrammed, so as to give you the chance to apply SQ$_3$R to some normal text material. (I would suggest you *recall* between four and six times on your way through.)

Please go on to make your preliminary *survey* of chapter 4.

4 How to Write Papers
(Study Time: about 25 minutes)

THE VALUE OF PAPERS

For many students paper writing is the bane of their lives. They question the usefulness of papers, make a big deal of writing them, and generally try to put off the task for as long as they can get away with it.

This is most unfortunate, for the writing of a paper can help the student in three ways:

1. It forces you to organize your thinking and come up with your own point of view on a topic.
2. It enables you (and your teacher) to recognize strengths that you must build on and weaknesses that you must remedy if you are to succeed in the course.
3. It gives you practice that will be useful in examinations (since most examinations still call for the ability to write short essays).

Of these three benefits, perhaps the greatest is the first. After we've read, heard, and talked about a topic, our minds are awash with ideas and impressions. But we never really come to grips with this experience unless we try to write it down. It is only when we come to put words on paper that we are forced to make these ideas precise, weigh them, reject those that are irrelevant, and organize the rest into a sensible pattern that we can call our own. *Writing is the crucial step* without which the process of study is incomplete. (And since practically every occupation you might enter will demand the same ability to report in writing, it is clearly a "life skill.")

UNDERSTANDING THE TASK

Many difficulties in writing a paper or an essay arise because the student has not planned it carefully enough or has not really thought about what the essay requires of him or her. He or she is only interested in getting it out of the way as quickly as possible.

When your teacher gives you an essay theme or paper title, take it down exactly, and examine the *precise* wording: what is demanded of you? Does the question or title call for a general treatment or for specific cases, a broad outline or a detailed account? Are you expected to state your own personal experience and opinions or simply to demonstrate your knowledge of other people's? Are you asked to refer to any particular sources of information or experimental data? Are you expected merely to describe things as they are (or were) or must you analyze and explain why they came to be that way? Do you need to discuss implications and suggest applications?

COLLECTING YOUR MATERIAL

Once you have decided on the nature and scope of the paper you have to write, it is time to do some research into its subject matter. Normally, you will need to go to a variety of sources for the material out of which you will shape your essay.

Questions

Whatever you do, don't just grab a pile of books and begin reading in the vague hope that something useful will jump out at you. Such browsing would be a waste of your precious time. To get results you must read *purposefully,* and the best way of ensuring this (as I've said before) is to have a set of specific questions that you want answered.

Now obviously you'll have an essay question (or paper title) but this is too broad—it needs breaking down before you can begin any useful research. The best way of breaking it down is to ask yourself questions about it. These questions can then guide you in your reading.

For instance, suppose you were asked to write on "The Use of Programmed Learning in Education and Industrial Training." You might begin by analyzing the title and coming up with a set of questions like these:

1. What is programmed learning? How long has it been in use?
2. Who uses it most, education or industry? Why?
3. Do they use it in similar ways or differently? Why?
4. How does it compare with other forms of learning? What sort of results does it get? What do students think of it? Are there any difficulties attached to using it?
5. Will it be more used or less used in the future? Will it be used in new ways? Will even newer methods take its place?

And so on.

Always try to think out (and write down) a few questions in this way before you begin your research for a paper. As you read, you will come up with further questions, more specific questions, and perhaps some of those on your original list will seem less relevant; but to have at least some questions to answer, right from the start, is an invaluable aid in research. The more clearly you know what information you are looking for, the more effectively you will read. So you'll save yourself a good deal of time.

Start Early

Start doing this preliminary thinking, and writing down your research questions, as early as possible after hearing the title of your paper. Even if a professor gives you a month or more, do some thinking right away: don't wait until the week before your deadline.

There are two very good reasons for at least making a start immediately:

1. In classes or in casual conversation, and especially in your general study reading, you may quite accidentally come across ideas that will be relevant to your paper. If you have not already given some thought to your topic, you

may miss many of these ideas and end up having to reread the texts merely because you didn't realize their significance the first time.

2. We all know how often we get a brilliant idea on a topic at a moment when we are thinking about something entirely different. The unconscious mind seems to go on chewing away at a problem even though we have turned our attention to other matters. So the more time you can leave between your first thinking about your paper and the day when you finally write it up, the more chance you are giving your unconscious mind to get a hold of new ideas and discover new relationships.

Keep a Notebook

It is wise to keep some sort of notebook with a page or so devoted to each paper or project that you have in the works at any one time. Then, if an idea occurs to you, or if you come across a useful quotation or illustration, or if you think of a piece of research to be followed up later, you can secure it down on paper before it fades from memory. Many successful students (and authors) claim they owe much of their success to the habit of always having such a book in their pockets and never letting a good idea escape unrecorded.

Sources of Information

Now where do you start looking for the answers to your research questions—the answers that will help you shape up your paper? Your major source of ideas is likely to lie in *reading*.

Possibly your professor, when he or she sets the paper topic, will give you a basic list of books and periodicals. And when you begin looking at texts from this bibliography you will probably find that they in turn suggest further books and articles that might be helpful to you. You may get useful ideas from textbooks, biographies, reference books and encyclopedias, research papers, scholarly journals, government reports, newspaper clippings, and so on. If you have trouble tracking down the right references, your college library staff will be glad to advise you. (Ask them to explain the library's system and resources—one of the most valuable things you can learn in college is how to make the best use of a library.)

Don't neglect the less formal sources of information, however. While the plan for the paper is germinating in your mind you should be alert for useful ideas that crop up unexpectedly in lectures, seminars, and tutorials, in your own personal experience, and in casual discussions with fellow-students or with teachers.

Record Your Sources

Whatever the sources of your ideas, make note of them. In writing down any idea that you think may have a bearing on your paper, record the title and author of the book or article (and who published it, when, and where), or the name of the speaker from whom you heard it. You *must* give credit to these sources if you use them in your paper. It creates a very bad impression with your professor if, through careless-ness or lapse of memory, you later present him or her with ideas as if they were your own but which he recognizes as coming from other authors (especially if your professor is one of them!).

PLANNING THE PAPER

Never jump straight from research into writing the first sentence of your paper. Too many papers start off in a flurry of enthusiasm only to fizzle out a few paragraphs later through lack of a sense of direction. Think your paper through before you write a word. That is, make a *plan*.

Selection of Material

The first step in planning is to weigh, and select from, the material you have collected in your research. You may have pages of notes. Which of them are relevant? Avoid the amateurish habit of trying to "work them all in somehow." Not all your ideas will be equally useful when you get down to shaping your paper. Some will seem trivial. Others will seem obscure. Yet others will be unsupported by sufficient evidence. These must be discarded. You will have no space for indecision, padding, or half-truths.

At the same time, remember that you will need examples to back up any statements of fact or opinion that you'll be making in your paper. Such material is not padding; indeed it is vital to the credibility and strength of your argument. Also, be sure that you have enough material to give due weight to *all* aspects of the paper. (Students often ignore the "reasons" or "implications" they were asked to discuss.)

What you must do is *select* just the most appropriate material for your paper, enough to cover it fully but not too much to confuse the issue. Having done this, and once you are sure of your facts and your sources, you can start arranging your ideas logically so as to make the greatest impact in your paper.

Write an Outline

The next step in planning your paper is to work out the basic structure or *outline*. Doing this has several advantages:

1. It helps you sort out what are the main ideas and the important details.
2. It makes sure you leave out nothing vital and that you don't repeat yourself.
3. It allows you, once started, to write fluently without having to keep chewing your pen and wondering what to say next.
4. If you are in an examination and time runs out, you may well gain more points from submitting a clear outline than you would from a half-finished essay.

*A **basic framework**.* Here is a three-point plan that you may have used before but which still is useful as a framework for a wide variety of papers:

1. *Introduction*
   A. Comment on subject of paper. (What do you understand by it? How is it important? etc.)
   B. Which aspects you will deal with and why. (Remember you can't say everything about anything in just a thousand words or so.)
2. *The Main Body*
   A. Develop your line of argument through three or four main ideas.

    B. Support each main idea with examples and illustrations drawn from experience or other authors.
3. *Conclusion*
    A. Summary of main ideas.
    B. Firm or tentative answer to question; or comment on topic of paper, indicating wider implications or future trends, or scope for further consideration.

I have already suggested (frame 3.25) that your job in reading should be to uncover the writer's outline of ideas (as I hope you are now uncovering *my* outline for this chapter). Before writing, of course, your job is just the opposite—to plan an outline for your own ideas. (One useful form of outline is shown in frame 7.8. Please look at it now.)

Start at the End

With a carefully planned outline and the notes you have made from your research, you should be able to start writing your paper. However, many students would suggest taking one final step in the planning: they would advise you to write the *last* paragraph of your paper first. We can justify this on two grounds:

1. It gives a sense of direction to your writing if you know exactly what conclusion you're heading toward.
2. It helps insure that your paper will conclude firmly and definitely, rather than just stopping lamely as so many do.

Perhaps you can summarize the theme of your paper in just one sentence: for example, "Programmed learning is still in its infancy and, while at present used more in industry than in education, its benefits are bringing it rapidly growing acceptance in both fields." If you can write such a summary sentence, then you could use it as the topic sentence of your final paragraph.

WRITING THE PAPER

Having selected the important ideas, made an outline, and written your final paragraph, you can begin writing your paper. But regard this as your first, trial draft. As one writer once said: "The best reason for putting anything down on paper is that one may then change it." Write as well as you can, but be prepared to make changes later. At this stage you should be more concerned with getting your ideas down somehow than with the best possible wording. You'll know better what you want to say when you see what you've written!

Style

Style is nothing more than the words with which you choose to express your thoughts. If your thoughts are woolly and confused, then your style will be also, and your essay will be difficult to read and understand. If, on the other hand, you have a clear picture of what you are trying to say and you know exactly where your argument is leading, then you should be able to write clearly and directly in a way that is easy for a reader to follow.

It is always best to write as simply and straightforwardly as possible. Use everyday language, but avoid slang. Write short sentences. Be concise: never write a paragraph when one sentence will do the same job.

Layout

Let the layout of your essay on the pages reflect the structure of your outline. If appropriate, use headings and subheadings within your essay. Split your work up into paragraphs: each main idea should have its own paragraph. All this helps your reader with *his* task.

Remember also that a picture can save you a great many words. Where a map or diagram or graph can save you writing a description, use it instead of words.

Make a clear distinction between your own ideas and those you've borrowed from other authors. Name your sources. If you are quoting other people's actual words, use quotation marks. Acknowledge any books or articles from which you have particularly drawn by writing a bibliography in the way I have done at the end of this chapter; and refer to these works by writing, for example, (Rowntree, 1983) after any reference or quotation within your essay.

REWRITING

Having written your paper you should put it aside for a few days. You need this time lapse to allow for the pride of authorship to subside. It is a great mistake to work so close to your deadline that you have no choice but to hand in the first draft as soon as it has come from your pen. Changes will almost certainly be needed.

Just a few days can give you quite a new perspective on your work. You will come back to it fresh, able to look at it more objectively, and you'll see a great many obscurities and pomposities that were not apparent to you in the heat of creation. In short, you will be able to assess it more *critically*—much as your reader will.

A Check List

Here are some useful questions to ask yourself about it:

1. Does the essay or paper answer the question or deal with the topic that was set?
2. Does it cover all the main aspects and in sufficient depth?
3. Is the content accurate and relevant?
4. Is the material logically arranged?
5. Is each main point well supported by examples and argument?
6. Is there a clear distinction between your ideas and those you have brought in from other authors?
7. Do you acknowledge all sources and references?
8. Is the length of the essay right for its purpose?
9. Is it written plainly and simply, without clumsy or obscure phrasing? (A good test is to *read it aloud.*)
10. Is the grammar, punctuation, and spelling acceptable, and is it neatly and legibly written?

Be strict with yourself on each of these points, since these are the questions your reader will ask him or herself in grading the essay. *Rewrite* your final draft so as to eliminate all the weaknesses you have spotted.

If you find it difficult to criticize your own work in this way, get a friend to examine your paper while you do the same for his. You will both learn from one another's comments. Teach yourself to look at your papers in the same way your reader will and you'll have gone a long way toward improving your grades.

Physical Appearance

Whatever you do, don't neglect the physical appearance of your paper. Make sure your final draft is neat, well laid-out, and either clearly handwritten or, preferably, *typed*. First impressions are very important in so subjective a job as grading an essay, and sloppy work suggests sloppy thinking. However unfair it may seem, teachers are only human, and they tend to be impatient with papers that are difficult to read: experiments have shown that bad handwriting can cost you one whole grade. It's no joke to get a B when legible writing could have earned you an A on the same paper. You have been warned!

By the way, papers do occasionally get lost after being handed in to a teacher. Carbon paper or xeroxing is cheap and easy insurance against the inconvenience and aggravation this might cause you. Whether you type or write by hand, always make a copy of your final draft.

One final point: Never be too anxious to get a paper out of the way. It's probably when you are most fed up with it that you are on the verge of producing something really worthwhile. Try to look on it not as a chore to be disposed of, nor as an obstacle to be overcome, but as a means of sharpening your thinking and as a personal expression of how well you understand.

Bibliography

Flesch, R. (1949). *The Art of Readable Writing* (New York: Harper & Row).

Maddox, H. (1978). *How to Study* (New York: Fawcett). (Chapter 10 on Writing English.)

Strunk, W. and White, E. B. (1978). *The Elements of Style,* 3rd ed. (New York: Macmillan).

4.1 Now:

1. Complete your *recall* of the chapter and make sure you have some notes. (I'll show you my own notes on the chapter as a check, later.)

2. *Review* the chapter.

Then tackle the review questions that follow.

REVIEW QUESTIONS

4.2 (If you need to refresh your memory, turn back to the *page* number mentioned.)

What are the *five* stages in producing an essay or paper? (Pages 58–65)

Understanding the task, collecting the material, planning the paper, writing the paper, and rewriting it.

4.3 Before you begin your *research* for a paper you should examine the title and work out a set of _____s to guide you. (Page 59)

---

question

4.4 If you have the title of a paper to be completed ten weeks from now, when would be the best time to start thinking about it? Why? (Pages 59–60)

Now. The longer the problem can simmer in your unconscious, the better; and you must be alert right away for relevant ideas that crop up in other work and may save you labor later on.

4.5 What are the steps (at least two) in *planning* a paper? (Pages 61–63)

Selecting your material, writing an outline, and (perhaps) writing a draft of the final paragraph.

4.6 Would you say the *style* of the chapter you have just read would generally be suitable for writing a paper? What word would you use to describe such a style? (Page 64)

Your opinion is what I asked for. Mine is that such a style (plain, simple, direct, natural) is suitable for most papers.

4.7 If you are using the ideas or the actual words of *other* writers within your paper, what steps will you take to let your reader know this? (Page 61)

Use quotation marks, name the other authors, write a bibliography.

4.8 In *re*writing your paper (producing the final draft) you should try to examine it from *what* point of view? (Pages 65–66)

From the point of view of the reader it is intended for.

4.9 Does it really make any practical difference whether or not your handwriting is clearly legible and your paper set out neatly on the page? Explain. (Page 66)

It does matter, because scruffy-looking work will almost certainly cost you points, and it will also be more difficult for you to revise from later.

4.10 Go on to chapter 5 (and don't forget to SURVEY it before you begin reading).

5 How to Read Better and Faster
(Study Time: about 50 minutes)

5.1 Most college students have been reading for a dozen years or more, yet few do it as well as they might. They read too slowly, they can't concentrate, and they don't remember what they've read. Since reading plays so large a part in a student's work, she clearly stands to gain if she can learn to do it with greater speed and comprehension.

BETTER READING

The first essential is to improve *comprehension*. How can you get a better understanding of a text, and remember it once you have read it?

The best way, as we have already decided, is to apply the SQ₃R method. (This will make your reading *active* and *purposeful*.)

That is, you should not begin reading a chapter until you have _____ed it, and asked _____s about it; and once you have _____ it you should try to _____ what you have read, and then _____ it.

survey   question   read   recall   review

5.2 The effective reader is the one who is reading purposefully with questions to be answered.

N.B. Have you surveyed this chapter and asked yourself questions about it yet?

In any intensive reading of a text (whether book, chapter, article, report, etc.) you will probably be trying to:

1. Find the *main ideas.*
2. Pick out *important details.*
3. *Evaluate* what you are reading.

Main Ideas

As we discussed in the chapter on SQ_3R, main ideas can be found at the level of the *book,* the *chapter,* the *section,* and the *paragraph.* You will *already* have got some grasp of the more general main ideas from your preliminary survey.

At the *read* stage you will be looking chiefly for the main idea in each _____ .

---

paragraph

5.3 *Topic sentences.* Most writers put just one main idea in each paragraph, and your job is to find it. Usually this main idea is stated in *one* sentence—called the *topic* sentence.

Very commonly, the writer *starts* his paragraph by stating the main idea. He then illustrates it, supports it, or elaborates on it in the rest of the paragraph.

So the topic sentence is often the _____ sentence in the paragraph.

So the topic sentence is often the first sentence in the paragraph. (It contains the main idea.)

5.4 Sometimes, however, the writer feels it will be more effective to *lead up* to the main idea rather than start out with it. In this case, he or she will hold back the topic sentence until the end of the paragraph. The major point of the paragraph will come in its *final* sentence.

Which sentence carries the main idea of the paragraph above?

The first.	**A**
The second.	**B**
The last.	**C**

5.5 **A.** *The main idea there was that a paragraph may have its major point in its last sentence. Now the sentence you picked out says that a writer often prefers to lead up to his main idea. Does this necessarily mean that he leaves it until the very end of the paragraph? No, it does not; so this sentence does not carry the main idea of that paragraph. Please take another look at frame 5.4.*

B. *Almost, but not quite. The main idea there was that a paragraph may have its major point in its last sentence. The sentence you have picked out says that a writer may hold back his topic sentence until the end of a paragraph. But this doesn't necessarily mean that he makes it the very last sentence, does it? And if you look at the paragraph again, you'll see that one of its sentences openly states the main idea leaving no doubt about it. Please look at frame 5.4 again.*

C. *The paragraph you looked at begins by saying that a writer often prefers to lead up to his main idea, and that he may leave his topic sentence until the end of the paragraph. But, as you say, it is the final sentence that neatly states the main idea. Please go on to frame 5.6.*

5.6 Normally, then, the _____ sentence (carrying the main idea) is either the _____ or the _____ in the paragraph.

---

topic   first   last

5.7 Very rarely will you find the topic sentence in the middle of a paragraph. But what you will come across, from time to time, is the kind of paragraph in which no single sentence can be said to carry the main idea. Particularly in fiction, or in paragraphs of descriptive writing, the essential idea may be spread out across the whole paragraph, or never stated explicitly at all.

But in the normal textbook or article, you will expect to find the _____ _____ contained in the first or last sentence.

---

main idea

Important Details

5.8 As well as picking out the main ideas, you'll need to have your eyes open for important details. Some students complain that they can find the main ideas but not the significant details. Others are so impressed by the details they can't see the main ideas. Yet others just can't tell the difference.

As I mentioned while we were discussing SQ$_3$R, it sometimes pays to _____ a chapter a *second* time in order to pick out the important details.

---

read

5.9 Just what is an important detail? It is one that clarifies, or supports, or illustrates, or develops the main idea. It may be an example, a proof, an explanation, an implication. Usually there is at least one important detail attached to each main idea.

Frame 5.7 has a paragraph in it. Look back now, and pick out:

1. The main idea.
2. One important detail.

---

1. *"The main idea may be spread over all the sentences in a paragraph"* (or words to that effect).
2. *"Particularly in fiction and descriptive writing"* is the only important detail—an example.

5.10 Sometimes it is a matter of *opinion* as to whether a particular detail is significant or not. Ask yourself: Is this the best possible example (or proof, etc.) of the main idea? Does the main idea really *need* supporting, or proving, or illuminating?

If a detail does not seem very important, you will presumably not take note of it.

Look, for example, at the second-to-last paragraph in chapter 4 (paper writing)—the paragraph on page 66 beginning "Whatever you do":

1. What is the main idea?
2. What would *you* regard as important details?

---

1. *The main idea is that the physical appearance of a paper is worth some attention.*
2. *You might well have decided any or all of these details are important enough to note:*
    a. *three aspects of "physical appearance"—neatness, layout, legibility*
    b. *advisability of typing*
    c. *the human impatience of professors*
    d. *experimental evidence of the effects of poor handwriting.*

5.11 *Look for signposts.* One way of spotting important details (and of confirming main ideas) is to look out for the clues that the author has used to help you read. He may have used both *visual* and *verbal* signposts.
Consider the *visual* signposts first:

1. Words printed in *italics,* or
2. Words underlined, or
3. Words in **boldface** type.
4. The *numbering* of points (as in this list).
5. The *lettering* of points (a, b, c, etc., as in the list at the top of the frame).

Which of these five kinds of clues have I used so far in this program?

I have used all the visual signposts except underlining and boldface type. (And my aim in using them was to draw your attention to main ideas and important details.)

5.12 You would be wise to keep equally alert for the author's *verbal* signposts. Look out for words and phrases like:

first	for instance
on the other hand	furthermore
however	therefore

Such words are the author's way of telling you that she is about to list details, contradict a point, introduce a qualification, give examples, add to the strength of her main idea, state a conclusion, and so on. They act as *links* between one section of her argument and the next, and should help you pick out the key ideas and significant details.

Can you see a "verbal signpost" of this kind in the first sentence of the paragraph above, beginning "You would be wise . . . ?"

"equally" (This verbal signpost links frames 5.11 and 5.12 by comparing the importance of the two kinds of signpost.)

5.13 *Diagrams and tables.* Many students miss a lot of main ideas and important details because they skip all the author's charts, graphs, tables, and diagrams. Some think the diagrams are just there for decoration; others fear they may be too difficult to understand.

Diagrams and comprehension

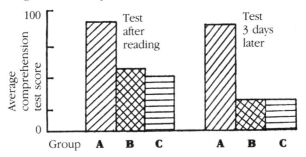

Average test scores of three groups of students after a reading experiment in which

Groups A and B were given a text with illustrations while Group C was given the same text with the illustrations removed and only **Group A** was told to pay special attention to the illustrations.

The truth is, an author's illustrations should be read as carefully as his text. He will certainly not have used them simply to liven up the page: space is too precious for that. A textbook author will only use tables and diagrams if he believes they will *teach better* than, and *instead of,* words.

So what is the *most important* reason for paying attention to the illustrations you come across in reading a book or article?

They may help you to a better understanding of the main ideas and important details you've read in the text. **A**
They may make it unnecessary for you to read the text at all. **B**
They may carry main ideas and important details that are not mentioned in the text. **C**

5.14 A. *Certainly this is one good reason for paying attention to tables and diagrams: they may clarify something in the text. However, it is not the* most *important reason. Please return to frame 5.13 and consider the alternatives again.*

B. *This is very unlikely. An author rarely gets enough space for all he wants to say; so he's not going to waste paper making every point both in words* and *in pictures. If you read only the pictures you'll miss some of his points, because some of them are made in words only. (Likewise, some points are made in pictures only.) Please return to frame 5.13 and reconsider the alternative answers.*

C. *Sometimes a picture saves a thousand words; sometimes it just saves a couple of dozen. But the author will rarely have space to repeat in print what he's already said very effectively with a diagram or table. Thus, the reader who skips illustrations may well be missing main ideas and important details that are not mentioned elsewhere in the text. Please go on to frame 5.15.*

5.15 So please don't regard an author's illustrations as mere decoration. But nor should you ignore them out of fear they may be difficult to read—they are rarely as complex as they may appear at first sight.

Difficulties. This goes for most difficulties in reading—whether with words or pictures. Try not to skip over them in the hope that they won't matter. If you leave a difficulty unconquered you may:

1. lose confidence and begin to feel uneasy, and
2. be prevented from understanding later ideas.

So, if you come to an *important* paragraph or diagram that you just can't make head or tail of, what should you do about it?

a. Forget about it and move on to more important material, or
b. Think extra hard about it, and even ask the advice of friends or teachers, or
c. Come back to it later, once you've mastered the rest of the text.

---

b. (To forget about a difficulty, temporarily or permanently, would probably run you straight into further difficulties with the text.)

5.16 Now, *without looking back,* just check how much attention you paid to the illustration I showed you in frame 5.13. Try to answer these questions:

1. How many groups of students took part in the reading test?
2. How did the groups differ in the way they worked?
3. Which group scored best on the test right after the reading?
4. Which group scored worst?
5. Was the score of the second-best group closer to the best group's score or to that of the worst group?
6. Does the experiment suggest that all students pay attention to diagrams whether told to or not?
7. Did the group that scored best on the first test also score best on the retention test three days later?
8. Whose score had changed most: that of the best group or that of the other groups?

Well, that should be about enough to make my point. Please go back and *check* your answers (and decide the answer to any question that stumped you). Then, when you are ready, go on to frame 5.17.

Let's hope you either (a) did quite well on that spot check, or (b) resolved to keep a sharper eye on the illustrations another time.

Evaluate the Text

5.17 So *quality* of understanding depends on how well you can sort out the main ideas and important detail from the text you are reading. But it also depends on your ability to *evaluate* what you read.

By this I mean you should be a *skeptical* reader. Force the author to prove all his statements. Look for limitations, exceptions, contradictions, arguments against those he puts forward. Ask:

1. Are his facts correct?
2. Does he distinguish between facts and opinions?
3. Do his conclusions follow from the facts?
4. Would other conclusions follow equally well?
5. Do his conclusions agree with yours/your professor's/other writers'?

To do all this you really have to come to grips with the book and relate all it says to your own experience. Look for your own *examples* and *applications* of what the author says.

What am *I* most concerned with in this book?

a. Having you remember my main ideas and important details so you can repeat them later in a test or exam.
b. Having you think critically about my suggestions and look for ways you might use them in your own work.

---

b. (I hope you are looking for applications for what I say, and are weighing my remarks according to whether or not each one might be of use to you in your own studying.)

5.18 So far we have dealt with the factors affecting your quality of comprehension in reading. But understanding is not the only thing required from the effective reader.

FASTER READING

How long have you taken to read this program so far? Whatever your answer, the odds are it's 50 percent bigger than it need be. Most of us could read *half as fast again*—and still understand just as well.

The average adult reads at about 240 words per minute. But with a little training anyone should be able to raise this, without loss of comprehension, to about _____ words per minute.

---

360 words per minute (that is, about six words a second)

Eyes and Brain

5.19 So why is it one person reads faster than another? And how can one increase one's speed? To answer these questions we need to consider what the eyes and brain are doing while we "read." To begin with, we all know that the eyes travel along a line of print from left to right (as yours are presumably doing now).

But how would you *describe* this movement from left to right?

a. a smooth, continuous sweep, or
b. a jerky, intermittent motion.

---

b. a jerky, intermittent motion. (Watch someone's eyes while he reads if you doubt this: you'll notice the split-second pauses.)

5.20 *Fixations.* The fact is that the brain can only recognize words when the eyes are still. So the eyes move along a line of print in a series of jerks, and after each jerk they stop briefly—they *fixate* on a piece of the text. (Your eyes may have made half a dozen such fixations in scanning the line above.)

At which points, then, is the brain "reading" words? Is it . . .

a. at each fixation? or
b. between fixations? or
c. both?

---

a. at each fixation (lasting perhaps ¼ second)

5.21 ***Recognition span.*** Now at each fixation only about four *letters* will be in sharp focus. If you look at the word "read" you see all the letters quite clearly. The words on either side ("word" and "you") will be out of focus, and therefore less clear, but your brain will still recognize them.

The number of words you can recognize at one fixation is called your *recognition span.* If you couldn't see any words to either side of "read," your recognition span would be one word—rather small. More likely, however, you'll be able to see two or three words at one glance. Some people, indeed, can take in a whole line at once, and thus read straight *down* a printed page.

Such people have an exceptionally large _____ _____ .

---

recognition span

5.22 So, when reading, your eyes move in a series of jerks interrupted by fixations. The number of fixations you need for a line of print will depend on how wide your recognition span is—how much of the line you can take in at once.

The bigger your recognition span, the *(more/fewer?)* fixations you'll need, and the *(faster/slower?)* you'll read.

---

fewer   faster

Poor Readers

5.23 The trouble with poor readers is that they have *small* recognition spans, so they are slowed down by the large number of fixations they have to make.

The illustration below shows how a good reader and a poor reader might view the same couple of lines of print. Each vertical mark indicates a point of fixation (numbered to show the order in which it was made):

```
         1            2         3      4       5         6
A. The unconscious mind seems to go on chewing away at a
```

7   8   9   10   11
problem even though we have turned| our attention to

12   13
other matters.

B.   1   2 5 3   6 4   7   8 10 9 13 11 12
    The unconscious mind seems to go on chewing away at a

14 15 16 17 20 18   19 24 21   22 23   25
problem even| though|we have turned our|attention to

26 27 28
other |matters.

1. Which is the *poor* reader? A or B?
2. Altogether he makes about *(how many times?)* as many fixations as the good reader.
3. Partly this is due to his small _____ _____ .
4. N.B. But it is also partly due to the fact that he has several times looked *back* along the line to fixate on something he has already "seen." This has happened _____ or _____ times in each line.

---

1. *B* is the poor reader.
2. *twice* as many fixations.
3. small *recognition span.*
4. *two* or *three.*

5.24 Regressions. As you might guess from that last example, the poor reader has never really got beyond elementary school reading ("read every word slowly and carefully") and he is still a "word-by-worder." In fact, he pays such individual attention to each word that he loses track of the overall meaning, and often forgets the beginning of the sentence before he gets to the end. So he can't keep his eyes moving (even slowly) from left to right: he has to move them back again to see what he's missed. These backward eye movements are called *regressions.*

As you noticed in the previous frame, the poor reader made at least two regressions per line, while the good reader made none at all.

Does a *good* reader *ever* make regressions?

Yes, but only when he is reading very difficult or badly written material.

5.25 *Vocalizing.* There is one more fault common among poor readers (and another hangover from elementary school days)—they *talk* themselves through a book. Of course, when we were first learning, we all used to read aloud. (Now we rarely do so except when entertaining other people or when consciously savoring the language of a text.) With practice, we have learned to read silently: but some people do it by talking to themselves. Even if they don't actually say the words aloud, they still go through the motions— moving their lips or making almost unnoticeable "subvocal" movements in the throat.

Would you think this affects the *speed* of the reading, or the *quality,* or *both,* or *neither?*

Speed certainly suffers. It is difficult to read any text aloud at more than about 125 words a minute, while a fairly average "silent" reader can manage more than 150 words a minute on a textbook and up to 600 words per minute on a novel.

Quality also suffers, because the "vocalizing" reader pores over one word at a time and so tends to lose sight of the sense of the sentence as a whole.

5.26 So we have picked out four faults associated with poor (slow and fuddled) reading:

1. Small recognition span
2. Many fixations
3. Frequent regressions
4. Vocalizing

Now let's stop pretending that these faults belong exclusively to other people. We *all* suffer from one or more of them, even if only from time to time and in certain kinds of reading matter. We are all slower than we need or should be.

Think a moment about each of these four faults. How would you set about *getting rid of one* if you found it occurring in your own reading?

See if you've anticipated any of the ideas I mention in the next few frames:

FIVE WAYS TO IMPROVE YOUR READING

5.27 To begin with, is it time you wore glasses for reading? Unless you've had an eye test in the last two years, set up an appointment to visit an *ophthalmologist* (not just a seller of glasses)—your college health service will help you find one. Many a student's reading problems have vanished once he or she has discovered (or admitted) a need for glasses.

There are many obvious signs of eye defects: blurring and dancing of the print; tilting of the head and twisting of the face while reading; blinking and watering of the eyes; inflamed eyelids; and headaches after reading for just a short while. But even the inability to concentrate *may* indicate a defect that could be corrected by wearing glasses for reading.

If you had such a defect, what difference *(increase or decrease)* might a pair of glasses make to:

1. The size of your recognition span?
2. The number of fixations you make?
3. The number of regressions you make?
4. The number of words you say aloud to yourself?
5. Your reading speed?
6. Your understanding?

---

1. *increase*
2. *decrease*
3. *decrease*
4. *decrease*
5. *increase*
6. *increase*

5.28 Second, *stop talking* to yourself. If you suspect you sometimes move your lips while reading, put your finger on them. This will both make you aware of the fault and prevent you from doing it.

But perhaps the best way of overcoming the habit is to read so _____ that your lips just can't keep up with you!

---

fast (Although it may be rather circular advice, one way of learning to read faster is to start reading faster.)

5.29 Third, then, *practice* reading faster. Stay alert, read with a sense of purpose, anticipate what you are about to read, and aim to get your eyes along that line of print as fast as possible. Don't regress to linger over something you've missed.

After all, which of these two approaches (if you were to spend an equal time on either) would be likely to give you the *better understanding* of a passage?

Reading *each word* slowly and carefully, looking *back* to previous phrases to check points you weren't sure about.   **A**

Reading the passage *twice* at something *close* to your top speed.   **B**

5.30 A. *This may sound like the safe and sure method, but I think you'd be disappointed with its results. Please glance back at frame 5.24 to remind yourself of the effects of word-by-word reading. Then read paragraph B below.*

B. *If you have any doubts at all about this "speed" approach, try it out when you next have the opportunity. You will find that even though you miss points on first reading (at just under your top speed) you will pick them up the second time around (in fact you may even manage a third "quick read" in the time it would have taken you to trudge laboriously from word to word). Go on to frame 5.31.*

5.31 Fourth, read in *thought-units*. Stop reading word-by-word and look instead for the way words *group* themselves within each sentence. You should aim to read each group or "thought-unit," at one glance. Indeed, your recognition span should take in a complete thought-unit.

A thought-unit may be a noun and its adjective, a verb and its adverb, or a short phrase, and so on. The thought-units in the last sentence of the previous paragraph are (to my mind): "Indeed—your recognition span—should take in— a complete—thought-unit." You don't have to read ten separate words in that sentence; you can swallow it in five gulps.

What are the major thought-units in the sentence you are reading right now?

Here is how I read the sentence:
"What are—the major—thought units—in the sentence— you are reading—right now?" (Is this more or less how you saw it?)

5.32 The good reader takes in about two words at one fixation in difficult material and three or more if the material is easy. By looking for thought-units he widens his recognition span and thus speeds up his reading.

Your recognition span depends also on one other very important factor (which you can definitely do something about). Read through the two sentences (1 and 2) below and decide:

a. Which of them can you read *more quickly* (with fewer fixations and regressions)?
b. Why is your recognition span *different* for each of the two sentences?

1. "Her Hengest and Aesc his sunu gefuhton with Bryttas, on thaere stowe the is gecweden Creccanford, and thaer ofslogon feower thusenda wera."
2. "At this time Hengest and Aesc, his son, fought against the Britons at the place which is called Crayford and slew four thousand men."

Both sentences said exactly the same thing, but unless you are fluent in Anglo-Saxon, you:

a. *Probably read (2) with fewer regressions and fixations.*

(That is with larger recognition span, and thus more quickly.) And:

b. *Your recognition span for* (1) *was smaller because you were* unfamiliar *with many of the* words *used.*

5.33 This brings us to the last, and very important, way of improving your reading skills.

Fifth, build up your *vocabulary*. The good reader knows a lot of words. She therefore reads not only with greater understanding, but also *faster,* because . . .

a. she can stop and consider the exact meaning of every individual word? or
b. she can take in the meaning of several words at a glance?

---

b. (The reader with a big vocabulary can take in the meaning of several words at one glance and thus can read faster.)

5.34 How big is *your* vocabulary? As a test, look at the words in the list below, which has been compiled from newspaper and magazine articles, a novel, biography, and a work of social reportage (Kirkman, 1967).
Ask yourself:

1. Could I *spell* each word correctly if I heard it read aloud?
2. Could I write each word in a *sentence* that would clearly show its meaning? (Use a dictionary if you need to check.)

complacent	reticence	inertia
emissary	dissemination	articulated
artefact	jeopardy	ubiquity
paradoxical	synthesis	tentative
misdemeanor	aberration	empirical
proliferate	omniscience	abstruse
unimpeachable	tenable	intuitively
autonomous	ostensibly	lucid
eradicate	atrophy	infallible
deducible	intractable	statutory
precursor	banality	intrepidly
insidious	collate	heretical
disparity	discern	immune
spectrum	anomaly	affluent

desultory	languid	adjacent
malignant	portent	dubious
infer	authentic	indigenous
scrutinize	inherent	disparagement
rationalist	propinquity	concomitants
unctuous	envisages	inexorably
efficacy	abject	precipitate (adj.)
altruism	indolence	transfiguring
categorically	caviling (at)	skeptical
depravity	exponents (of)	benefactor

Count the number of words whose *meaning* you *do not* know.

How did you score?
There were 72 words altogether. If you *missed*:

7 words or less	Quite likely you already read widely, quickly, and with clear understanding.
8 to 12	You probably have a reasonable vocabulary at this moment, but you should do all you can to keep it *growing*.
13 or more	You are almost certainly being held back by a weakness with words. You *must* give serious attention to increasing your vocabulary.

5.35 A wide vocabulary is essential, both for understanding other people's ideas (whether in speech or writing) and for expressing your own. Actually, of course, what we loosely speak of as *a* vocabulary is really *three* vocabularies (each of different size):

1. The words you use in speech.
2. The words you use in writing.
3. The words you understand in reading (and listening).

Which of these three vocabularies is the *largest*? Which is *smallest*?

Probably your reading vocabulary is largest and your speaking vocabulary smallest. (Most of us can recognize words in print that we would hesitate to try out in our writing, let alone in speech.)

Vocabulary Building

5.36 But how does one build up one's word-power? Here are six useful steps toward a bigger vocabulary:

1. Read *widely* (not just in your own subjects).
2. Learn some of the common *Latin and Greek roots* on which so many of our words are based. There is an entertaining *book* that will help you here (Davis, 1967).
3. Be on the *lookout* for new words, and *write them down.*
4. Get the *dictionary habit:* Look up and note the meaning of each new word as soon as possible after meeting it.
5. Use your new words in your writing (and speech) at the first suitable opportunity.
6. Make your own *glossary* for technical words and phrases that occur in your subjects.

So we've discussed five possible ways of improving your reading—from having your eyes tested to expanding your vocabulary. In which of the following *aspects* of reading would you expect to see such improvements:

a. Speed with which you read?
b. Understanding of what you read?
c. Memory of what you have read?

---

a   b   c
(All these aspects of reading would be likely to improve together.)

Practice Is Essential

5.37 If you want to improve your reading you must make a *conscious* effort, and practice regularly. Set aside fifteen to twenty minutes every day, perhaps just before you go to bed. For the first few days stick to light reading, say *Readers' Digest* (which does contain many *short* articles on a *variety* of topics); then tackle some long articles in newspapers like the *New York Times* or the *Christian Science Monitor,* and move on to magazines like *Time* or *Newsweek* or *National Geographic,* and then on to more textbook-like material once you've built up your stamina.

Tackle perhaps one or two articles every training session. Estimate the number of words in the article (fairly simple once you know the wordage of a full page or column), then see how quickly you can read it—time yourself to the nearest second.

Then try to *recall* what you've read—and check back through the article to see that you've picked out all the main ideas and important details. Don't worry if you miss a few at first, but keep trying to increase your speed *and* comprehension together. (This can all be a good deal easier, of course, if you can cooperate with a friend: each can then time the other and ask him or her questions about what he or she has read.)

Keep a record of your speed on each article you read (preferably in *words per minute*). Draw a chart if you need a morale-booster! Within a couple of weeks you should begin to see a marked improvement.

What *other opportunities* (besides these nightly half-hours) would you have for practicing faster and better reading?

Well I hope you'll be making a conscious effort to do all your study reading more rapidly. (After all, the purpose of the nightly sessions is to improve your reading skills for normal study; so why lose time before getting the benefits?)

Vary Your Pace

5.38 If you consciously strive, then, to increase your vocabulary and recognition span (and thereby make fewer fixations, and no regressions or subvocal noises) you will soon be able to read faster, with no loss of understanding.

But does this mean you will then tear through every bit of reading at exactly the same pace? No, it does not. Once you have learned to read faster you should be able to *vary* your speed according to what kind of material you are reading and what you are looking for. For instance:

1. With which reading *material* might you read more *slowly*?
   a. Novels, biography, and history, or
   b. Instruction manuals and textbooks.

2. For which reading *purpose* might you read more *slowly*?
   a. Looking for main ideas, or
   b. Looking for important details.

Probably: 1. *b*   2. *b*

5.39 So, whatever the nature and purpose of your reading, you
will try to do it as quickly as possible. But since you cannot
afford to sacrifice comprehension for speed, you will have to
vary your pace to suit the occasion.

This does not mean, however, that you will need to fall
back on word-by-word reading. If some material really does
give you trouble, remember you may profit more from
reading it several times at a little under your top speed than
from ploughing slowly through it once. Yet even though
you've taken in each paragraph quite quickly, you may still
appear to be slow over the chapter as a whole. Why? Because
you are not simply a recording machine. As a student—
someone who is looking for *meaning*—you will often need to
pause for thought between paragraphs, reflecting on the
relationships between what you are reading now and your
previous experience. All the same, with practice, your "slow"
reading speed may well turn out to be faster than what is now
your maximum.

Bibliography

Davis, N. (1978). *Vocabulary Improvement,* 3rd ed. (New
    York: McGraw-Hill).
Kirkman, A. J. (1967). "Command of Vocabulary Among Uni-
    versity Entrants" in *Education Research* IX2.
Leedy, P. D. (1963). *Read with Speed and Precision* (New
    York: McGraw-Hill).

N.B. Please *RECALL* this chapter (making some notes) and
REVIEW it before you go on.

Then tackle the review questions that follow.

REVIEW QUESTIONS

5.40 One basic way to improve reading is to make it active and purposeful by using the _____ approach. (Frame 2)

SQ_3R

5.41 While reading a text you will be trying to do *three* things. What are they? (Frames 1–2)

Find the main ideas, pick out important details, evaluate the text.

5.42 Where would you normally expect to find the *main idea* of a paragraph? (Frames 3–7)

In the first or last sentence.

5.43 What are the two kinds of "signposts" that can help the reader find the main ideas and important details? (Frames 11–12)

Visual (italics, underlining, etc.) and *verbal* (link words).

5.44 Why is it dangerous to skip the author's illustrations in reading? (Frames 13–16)

They may contain main ideas and important details that are not developed in the text.

5.45 State a question of the kind you might ask in *evaluating* a text. (Frames 17–18)

"Is this true?" is perhaps the most obvious question, but frame 5.17 lists several more, and you may have thought of yet others.

5.46 In the case of *poor* readers, which of the following tends to be *too large,* and which *too small?*

1. number of fixations
2. size of recognition span
3. number of regressions
4. amount of vocalizing

(Frames 23–26)

---

1. *too large*   2. *too small*   3. *too large*   4. *too large*

5.47 List five possible ways of improving speed and comprehension in reading. (Frames 27–36)

Get eyes tested; stop "talking"; practice reading faster; read in thought-units; increase vocabulary.

5.48 After regular practice in rapid reading, which of the following would you expect to be able to do?

1. Understand anything by reading at top speed.
2. Increase or decrease your reading speed according to circumstances.
3. Increase your average reading speed.
4. Keep up speed in future without further conscious effort.
5. Read everything at the same speed.

(Frames 37–39)

---

2 and 3

5.49 When you are ready, go on to chapter 6, a very brief one, and make a conscious effort to read it more rapidly than you normally would.

6 How to Learn from Group Discussion
(Study Time: about 15 minutes)

With some topics of study you may be able to make quite satisfactory progress by reading and writing about them, listening to lectures, and carrying out any necessary laboratory or fieldwork. This will be especially so, perhaps, in math- and science-based subjects. With many topics, however, especially in the arts and social sciences, you won't feel that you're getting your learning into perspective unless you have frequent opportunities to discuss the key issues with other students. You'll want to argue through the topics with your friends, exposing yourself to a variety of viewpoints and interpretations, and gaining both renewed enthusiasm and deepened understanding from the ebb and flow of discussion.

Opportunities for useful discussion may arise regularly and naturally in class work with your professor. He or she may leave ten minutes or so at the end of a lecture for questions and discussion. Or he may schedule sessions that are completely devoted to discussion of one kind or another. These may take many forms—from so-called simulation games to group problem-solving exercises. Let's look at just a couple of basic forms which, if the teacher doesn't arrange enough of, the students can easily organize for themselves. One of these two forms I'll call a "tutorial discussion" and the other a "seminar."

A TUTORIAL DISCUSSION

This can be lead by a professor, teaching assistant (usually a graduate student), or even a student who introduces the central topic or theme, arising perhaps out of a previous lecture or assignment, that the group is to consider. The group should be big enough to allow for a variety of knowledge and opinion, yet small enough to encourage and allow everyone to contribute—perhaps a dozen or so students at most. The atmosphere should be friendly and mutually supportive but all participants should have prepared in some way for the discussion. They must know enough about the topic to ensure that the discussion does not degenerate into either a lecture from the group leader or an uncontrolled swapping of unsupported prejudice.

There are several ways in which you can make best use of such a tutorial discussion:

1. Find out about the topic or theme in advance and read up on it.
2. Identify questions, issues, or contradictions that you would like to see aired in discussion.
3. Listen carefully to the opinions being expressed and the facts with which they are backed up; make occasional notes if this helps you concentrate.
4. Compare the facts with those known to you, and the opinions with your own. Challenge inaccurate or illogical statements—but politely!
5. If someone advances an opinion or argument that you don't understand, ask for it to be put another way.
6. Be prepared to ask questions or offer examples.
7. Put forward your own opinions for discussion. If your opinions are sound they will help others. If not, it's a good idea to get them out of your system before they become part of you.
8. If you know of an opinion or argument that would enrich or enliven the discussion, but which has not yet been raised, put it forward even if it is not your own.
9. Help the group to keep the topic or theme in mind and avoid straying too far into side issues that are of interest to a minority only.
10. Whenever you speak, keep to the point and be as succinct as possible. If the other members of the group want you to elaborate, they'll ask you.
11. Don't be afraid of thoughtful silences.
12. Encourage fellow-students who are having difficulty getting their ideas across.

13. If no one else is doing it, help the group from time to time by summing up progress to date (e.g., "We seem to agree on so-and-so, but disagree about such-and-such. Some say this while others say that. Is this a fair summary?") Such a summing up can be a valuable spring-board to further discussion, and knowing that you may need to provide it will certainly help you keep alert.
14. Make a few notes afterwards to remind you of the main lines of the discussion and the state of your own opinions at the end of it.

A SEMINAR

In a typical seminar a student reads a paper she has prepared on a topic of common interest (speaking perhaps for ten minutes or more) and then defends it in discussion with her fellow-students. The role of the group leader is simply to help keep the discussion to the point, to ask the occasional clarifying question, and perhaps, at the end, to sum up and throw in any opinions, references, or further evidence that have not been explored in discussion.

Clearly a seminar is of enormous benefit to the student presenting the paper. To do the job effectively she must select from a variety of data, prune and organize her ideas into a coherent thesis, and then present it logically and persuasively to her sympathetic but critical colleagues. True, a certain amount of mild tension is inescapable for the presenter if she really cares about what she is doing but, in the informal and friendly atmosphere of a seminar, the effect is often to give her a lucidity and persuasiveness that she wouldn't normally lay claim to! If you get a chance to prepare such a presentation, make the most of it: you'll thus ensure that you know at least one topic inside out.

It is possible to get almost as much benefit out of criticizing and commenting on a paper presented by someone else, provided you:

1. Read and think about the topic in advance.
2. Take an active part in the discussion along the lines suggested for a tutorial discussion.
3. Make some brief notes afterwards to sum up the speaker's main argument and the main points of discussion that followed.

DO IT YOURSELF

If "official" discussions don't occur as often as you and your
friends would like, then organize your own. Teachers do
not have to be present in order for learning to take place.
Students can undoubtedly learn a great deal from one
another. Provided all participants in a discussion prepare
adequately, and are able to admit that they do not know all
there is to be known about the topic, there is no reason
to fear that the blind will be led by the partially sighted. Nor,
provided they are willing to work for *one another's* understanding, need the situation be one where people think aloud
but don't actually listen to one another.

Either the tutorial discussion or the seminar form can be
followed, with a student appointed as chairperson in place
of a professor or teaching assistant. Appointing such a leader
probably is a useful formality, especially if the group contains
more than a dozen people. He or she can do a lot to ensure
that everyone contributes, that "super-stars" do not dominate
the discussion, and that the atmosphere stays reasonably
sweet! Actually, six to eight students is probably about the
right size for such a group. Much bigger and it might well
tend to splinter into factions whose members just talk among
themselves, anyway. Naturally, each member should be
expected to take his turn at each of the tasks associated with
the group—arranging the meeting, presenting a paper,
being chairperson, and so on. Hill's book (see below) gives
very useful advice about the roles that need to be performed
by group members and how to organize fruitful discussions.
See also what I have to say in chapter 8 about one special
kind of student-run group—the revision group.

Of course students also learn from each other in less
formal situations. Useful discussions often spring up in hall-
ways, in pubs, and on the bus going home. Even though
you may not, in any strict sense, have prepared for such
discussions, you should always be ready to participate as
actively as possible *and* to make a *note* of any important
points that emerge. (Remember the pocket notebook I
advised you to carry always? See page 60.) And don't forget
that students can learn from one another in groups of *two* as
well as in larger gatherings. You will soon become aware
of friends who have more grasp of a particular subject area
than you have and from whom you can occasionally seek

discussion and advice. Similarly, you should be prepared to give some of your time to advising fellow-students in those areas you are best at: not just out of natural kindness but also because the effort of sharing experience with someone else helps you get your own ideas sorted out.

Bibliography

Abercrombie, M. L. (1980). *The Anatomy of Judgement* (New York: Humanities Press).
Hill, W. F. (1977). *Learning Thru Discussion,* rev. ed. (Beverly Hills, Calif.: Sage).

6.1 How much do you RECALL after your first rapid reading of the chapter? For instance, what are the two main forms of discussion mentioned? How do they differ? Could you summarize the chapter's main points of advice in one sentence?

1. Write notes on what you remember.
2. Review the chapter (quickly), asking yourself the questions above. Then tackle the following review questions.

REVIEW QUESTIONS

6.2 I believe this short chapter makes *three* main points about how to ensure you get maximum benefit from discussion groups. What are they? (Briefly skim the chapter again if necessary.)

The three points (which are pretty well spelled-out in the section about seminars) are:
1. Prepare   2. Actively participate   3. Make notes afterwards.

6.3 About which of these three main points are you given most "important detail" in the chapter?

Eleven of the fourteen points listed in the section on tutorial discussions are important detail about how *to participate actively in a discussion (no. 2). You will perhaps find it useful to return and reread those points quite* slowly *(thinking about what they might mean for you) before you next take part in a discussion.*

6.4 One last question:
What is the minimum requirement for a useful discussion?

    a. One teacher and one student, or
    b. One teacher and two students, or
    c. Two students, or
    d. More than two students.

---

    c. Two students. (More students and a teacher will often be valuable but are not essential to useful discussion taking place.)

6.5 When you are ready, go on to chapter 7 (and don't forget to apply what you learned in chapter 5).

7 How to Take Notes
(Study Time: about 45 minutes)

THE VALUE OF NOTES

7.1 Poor or nonexistent note-taking is one of the common causes of failure for a student. Notes are a vitally important part of learning. Like the writing of papers and essays, they give you practice in "giving out" as well as "taking in."

Note-taking helps in two ways: First, it keeps you *active while* you are learning (thus aiding your concentration).

What is the *second* benefit you get (maybe weeks later) from having made notes?

You have a written record *from which you can* revise.

7.2 If you really want to get a grip on what you have heard or read it is far more valuable to put a few words on paper than to make do with a headful of hazy memories. The memories will soon drift away unless you pin them down in words, but you can keep your written record as a permanent reminder.

How to Store Notes

There are many ways of keeping your notes. Some will be more suited to your purpose than others. I describe below the practices of three different students.

Which of these methods would you consider most efficient?

a. Notes made on odd scraps of paper and the backs of envelopes; kept in a cardboard folder, or
b. Notes made on loose sheets of paper of uniform size; kept in a loose-leaf binder, or
c. Notes made and kept in a thick, hard-backed bound notebook.

Well I asked your opinion. I'm sure you scorned method a and made your choice between b and c. My own preference is for b—the loose-leaf binder. Although a bound notebook looks neater and easier to manage, it prevents you from arranging your notes in the most useful way.

7.3 Ideally you should be able to arrange your notebook so that *all* notes on a given topic are *together*—whether you got them from reading, lectures, or experiment, and whether you made them this term or last year. With a bound notebook, you are forced to store your notes in the order you wrote them, and the same topic may be dealt with in many different parts of the book. With a loose-leaf binder, on the other hand, you can reorder your pages, remove them, rewrite them, and add new material at any point you wish.

So, suppose you've just made notes on chapter 10 of a particular textbook. Where would you be most likely to store them?

a. In between the notes for chapters 9 and 11, or
b. Directly after the last set of notes you took, or
c. Along with notes from other sources dealing with the same topic as chapter 10.

---

c *I hope; a and* b *would be suitable places only if they happened to have notes on the* same topic *as chapter 10.*

WRITING THE NOTES

7.4 The main problem with notes is knowing what to put in and what to leave out. Working from books you get more time to make up your mind than you do in lectures but, ideally, the contents might be pretty much the same in either case.

Contents

Your notes should contain enough of the author's (or lecturer's) line of argument or discussion to bring it all clearly *back to mind* at a later date. Thus, your notebook must show:

a. The author's or lecturer's main ideas and any important supporting detail.
b. The logical plan of his or her argument (the hierarchy of ideas).

1. At *what step* of SQ$_3$R do you begin to get some inkling of the *logical plan* of the author's argument (by examining headings, etc.)?
2. At *what step* do you confirm this impression and pick out the *main ideas* and *important detail* (by looking for topic sentences, etc.)?

---

1. *survey* (and possibly *question*)   2. *read*

7.5 So, you should pick out the key ideas and the way they are organized in the course of surveying, questioning, and reading.

You will then make your notes at the _____ step of SQ$_3$R, and check them against what you have read as part of the _____ step.

---

recall (NOT *read*)   *review*

7.6 Don't try to make notes until you've finished reading a section. Too many students read with one finger tracing along the lines of their book while the other hand diligently copies down great chunks from the text. All they end up with is a mini-textbook: when it comes to revision they might as well reread the original.

Remember that you are trying to recall only the *essentials* of the author's argument or discussion. Your aim should be to capture on two or three pages what he has said in twenty or thirty.

How should you word your notes?

a. Stick as closely as possible to the author's words, or

b. Use your own words as much as possible.

N.B. Have you *surveyed* and asked *questions* about this chapter yet?

---

b. *(Mostly you should be using your own words—except where you need to record a specific quotation.) Your notes should be an expression of your understanding, not of your copying ability. Try not to look back at the author's words until you have sketched out some notes and are ready to review.*

Outline or Summary?

7.7 Broadly speaking, there are two ways of writing notes: as outlines or as summaries. While summaries are simply condensed versions of the original, still written in continuous prose, outlines (or skeleton notes) present the essential points in an almost diagrammatic fashion.

In the next two frames (frames 7.8 and 7.9) you'll see notes about chapter 5 of this book made by two different students:

1. Which frame shows notes in *outline* form? 7.8 or 7.9?
2. Which notes more clearly show up the *logical relationships* within the chapter? Outline or summary?
3. Which notes would you find easier to *revise* from? Outline or summary?

When you have decided your answers, please go on to frame 7.10.

7.8 Notes from *Learn How To Study* (ch. 5) by D. Rowntree 15/10/83

How to Read Better and Faster

  I. Despite "experience" few college students read as well as they might. (Too slow, can't concentrate, forget.)
  II. For *better* reading (improved comprehension):
    A. Apply SQ_3R to get sense of purpose.
    B. Look for topic sentence in each paragraph:
      1. Usually first or last sentence, and
      2. Contains the *main idea* of the paragraph.

C. Look for important *details*:
  1. e.g., proof, example, or support for main idea.
  2. Usually at least one to each main idea.
D. In hunt for main ideas and important details:
  1. Watch out for signposts:
    a. Visual (layout and typestyles).
    b. Verbal (clue words and phrases).
  2. Study all charts and tables.
  3. Don't skip difficulties.
E. *Evaluate* the text:
  1. Be skeptical. (Expect author to prove.)
  2. Look for applications in your own experience.

III. Toward *faster* reading: (Most people could read half as fast again and still understand just as well.)
  A. During reading:
    1. Eyes jerk left to right in series of *fixations.*
    2. At each fixation, brain decodes group of words,
    3. Making up its *recognition span.*
  B. *Poor* readers:
    1. Have small recognition spans.
    2. ∴ make many fixations.
    3. Regress frequently. (Backward glances.)
    4. Read aloud. (Or make subvocal noises.)

IV. Can improve reading. (Speed *and* understanding.)
  A. Five basic steps:
    1. Check whether you need glasses.
    2. Stop saying words aloud.
    3. Consciously try to read faster.
    4. Read in thought-units. (2 or 3 words at a time.)
    5. Build up vocabulary (reading, speaking, writing) by:
      a. Reading widely.
      b. Learning Greek and Latin roots.
      c. Noting new words.
      d. Using dictionary.
      e. Making glossaries.
  B. Practice (absolutely essential) by:
    1. Nightly sessions (15–30 min.).
      a. Read articles of known length.
      b. Time yourself (w.p.m.). (Progress chart?)
      c. Test your comprehension.
    2. Reading *all* study material faster.

C. Vary your reading pace:
1. Faster for "storylike" material and main ideas.
2. Slower for complex argument and for important detail.

Compare these notes with those in frame 7.9. Then return to frame 7.7.

7.9 Notes from *Learn How to Study* (ch. 5) by D. Rowntree
12/11/83

How to Read Better and Faster

Few college students have learned to read as well as they might: they read too slowly, they can't concentrate, and they don't remember what they have read. But they can usually improve by following some of these suggestions:

For improved comprehension, the reader should apply the SQ_3R approach which will keep him *active* and *purposeful*. He should look for the *topic sentence* (usually the first or last) in each paragraph, for it will carry the paragraph's *main idea*. He will also need to look for the *important details* (examples, proofs, etc.) that go to support the main idea. (Usually there is at least one important detail to every main idea.) In his search for main ideas and important details he should be alert for visual and verbal *signposts* (clues to the author's meaning) and should pay proper attention to all charts and tables and diagrams. He should not skip over difficulties. The reader should also aim to *evaluate* the text by reading skeptically and looking for applications of what he reads.

Most people could increase their reading speed by 50 percent without loss of understanding. During reading, the eyes move across the page from left to right in a series of quick jerks with stops (called *fixations*) in between: during the fixations, the brain registers a group of words *(recognition span)*. Poor readers have small recognition spans and therefore make many fixations. They also take many backward glances *(regressions)* over what they have already seen, and they sometimes tend to mouth the words or say them aloud. All these faults help to slow them down.

A student can usually improve both his speed and his understanding in reading: he should check whether he needs reading glasses, prevent himself from saying words aloud, try consciously to read faster, read in thought-units, and *increase his vocabulary.* He can increase his vocabulary by wide reading, learning Greek and Latin word roots, taking note of new words, using the dictionary, and making glossaries in his own subjects. Practice is essential and can be applied both to normal study reading and to regular nightly sessions. In these nightly sessions (¼-hour minimum) the student should read articles of known length, time himself, and calculate his speed in words per minute, and then test his understanding of the content. Once he has increased his ability to read at speed, he will be able to *vary* his reading speed to suit his material and his purpose: faster perhaps with novels, biography, and history, and when looking for main ideas; more slowly with instructional manuals, textbooks, and when looking for important details.

Compare these notes with those in frame 7.8. Then return to frame 7.7.

---

1. *Frame 7.8 shows an outline (7.9 a summary).*
2. *The outline shows up the relationships more clearly.*
3. *The outline is probably easier to revise from.*

7.10 *Writing an Outline.* Where possible, try to outline rather than summarize your reading and your lectures. Here's how to begin outlining a text:

Get a skeleton for your outline from the author's *headings* (if he has used them). Expand each heading into a *sentence* containing the main idea of the section or subsection it belongs to.

Especially when headings are few, you will also need to look at the topic sentence of each paragraph in the section. It probably carries a main idea that you will need to put in your notes to help develop the argument.

If you want to include *important details,* enclose them in *parentheses.*

Look back to frame 7.8 (and, if necessary, to chapter 5) to see how our student handled this in his outline. *What else* has he done—in order to show up the *logical plan* of the argument?

As you'll have noticed, the student did turn each of my headings into a sentence containing a main idea; he got further items for his outline from the topic sentences of my paragraphs; he put important details in parentheses. In addition—*to indicate the structure of the argument—he set his note-items* in from the *margin and added* letters *and* numbers.

7.11 So, having picked out the main ideas (of sections, subsections, and paragraphs), you *indent* them from the margin, according to their relative importance. Main items start *at* the margin. Second-order items are indented by, say, half an inch. Third-order items go in by another half inch, and so on.

Don't indent too little, or the relationships won't be clear. Don't indent too much, or you won't have room for your notes.

In the outline notes on frame 7.8 there are four main items, ten second-order items, twenty-five third-order items, and *(how many?)* fourth-order items.

---

ten fourth-order items. (II.D.1.a., IV.A.5.d., etc.)

7.12 As you've noticed, that last outline used not only indentation but *also* letters and numbers. To show how your notes hang together you need a system of lettering and numbering that will emphasize the relationships.
For example:

Main items	Roman numerals (large)	I, II, III, IV
2nd order	Capital letters	A, B, C, D
3rd order	Arabic numerals	1, 2, 3, 4
4th order	Lower-case letters	a, b, c, d
5th order	Roman numerals (small)	i, ii, iii, iv

And if you need extra orders you can always start putting parentheses around Arabic numerals (1), or around lower-case letters (a).

In the next frame you will see an outline for chapter 4 of this book. (In fact, it is the outline from which I *wrote* the chapter; but it is also the sort of outline you should be able to make from reading it.) However, I've left a few of the letters and numbers out. Will you please *complete the job.*

7.13 (*Did* your *notes for the chapter look anything like this?*)

How to Write Essays

I. Writing essays can help you in three ways:
 A. Forces you to organize your thinking.
 B. Shows up your strengths and weaknesses.
 C. Prepares you for exam situation.
II. Make sure you *understand* the essay task:
 A. What is the precise subject?
 B. What kind of treatment called for?
III. How to *collect* suitable material:
 A. Think out questions to guide your research.
 B. Begin thinking right away in order to:
  1. Make yourself alert for relevant ideas.
  2. Give unconscious mind a chance.
 C. Keep a notebook for essay ideas.
 D. Investigate all possible sources of information:
  1. Books, articles, etc. suggested by teacher.
  2. " " " " by those books (or library staff).
 E. Note the source of all materials you collect.
IV. Spend time *planning* the essay:
 A. Select the most useful of your material:
  1. Throw out the trivial, irrelevant, or obscure.
  2. But keep enough detail to support your argument.
 __ Write a logical outline.
  __ This ensures that you:
   __ Sort out the main ideas and important details.
   __ Miss nothing vital.
   __ Write fluently.
   __ Get extra points on exams.
  __ One basic outline framework is:
   __ Introduction—comment on subject and your treatment.
   __ Main body—your argument in 3 or 4 main ideas.
   __ Conclusion—summary and final comment.
 __ Write the final paragraph.

__ Write the *first draft* of your essay:
   A. Write simply and directly.
   B. Let layout reveal structure of argument.
   C. Use pictures if they can save words.
   D. Clearly distinguish your ideas from other people's.
   E. Write a bibliography.
VI. *Rewrite* the essay after a few days:
   A. Check for and eliminate weaknesses of content or treat-
      ment.
   B. Make sure final draft is neat and clearly written.
   C. Keep a copy.

When you have filled in the missing numbers and letters (12 of them altogether) turn to frame 7.14.

The numbers and letters you should have filled in are (in order):
B.   1.   a.   b.   c.   d.   2.   a.   b.
C.   C.   V.

7.14 So here is how to write good outline notes from a book:

   1. Expand the author's *headings* and restate *topic sentences*
      so as to get items that express the main ideas of sections
      and paragraphs.
   2. Write any important detail in brackets.
   3. Lay out your items using *indentation* to show which
      comes under which.
   4. Letter and number the items to make this relationship
      even clearer.

Now make a brief outline based on the first few headings (and some extra words and phrases) from chapter 3. (You'll need to glance back at the chapter.) Just *expand* the phrases below, *indent* them as you see fit, and *add* your numbers and letters.

SQ3R   SURVEY   **Surveying a Book**
Title page   Preface   Contents
Leaf through the book.   **Surveying a Chapter**
First and last paragraphs   Summaries
Headings
(Topics dealt with. How they relate. . .) Question

When you have finished your outline, check with frame 7.15.

Does your outline look anything like the one below?
SQ3R (survey, question, read, recall, review) is a useful approach to studying a text, and consists of the following steps:

I. *Survey* first to get a general view of what you will then study in detail:
- A. Survey the book as a whole.
  1. Glance at the title page.
  2. Read the preface.
  3. Examine the table of contents.
  4. Leaf through the book.
- B. Survey each chapter in more detail before you study it.
  1. Read the first and last paragraphs.
  2. Read any summaries.
  3. Examine the headings to discover:
- a. What topics are dealt with.
- b. How they relate to one another.

II. Look for *questions* that will give purpose to your reading.

7.15 Now the outlining method obviously gives you a very useful set of notes from which it is easy to revise—you can see the gist of the matter at a glance. I hope you'll find plenty of use for it in the future (if it isn't already your normal method).

Writing a Summary. But what about the summary? Are there some subjects or topics in which it would be preferable to write your notes in straight prose, in continuous paragraphs?

Can you think of any kinds of reading you do for which such *summary* notes might be *preferable*?

Of course your answer will depend on your subject, and the kinds of reading you have to do. Possibly in some parts of language learning, or mathematics, a summary will be preferable. Again, with literature or some aspects of history, you may find that what you need to refresh your memory is a synopsis, a summary, or even an appreciation or critique—written in continuous prose.

7.16 But if you do decide to write a prose summary, keep it short, and make it as easy to revise from as possible. This brings us to another important aspect of taking notes—how to set them down on the page.

The Mechanics of Note-taking

And the first question here is: How good is your *handwriting*? Will your notes be clear and readable to you, perhaps a year or more after you wrote them? (A recent survey at one university showed that more than 60 percent of the students had difficulty in reading their own notes.)

Obviously your notes will be no use to you if you can't _____ them. One way of making them more legible than even the best handwriting could, would be to _____ them.

---

read   type (The student who can type up his notes is at a considerable advantage: provided he *rethinks* them while he types.)

7.17 But even if you decide to use a typewriter you can't, of course, take it into lectures (or into examinations), so you'll still have to make sure your handwriting is reasonably legible.

Abbreviations. In lectures, particularly, your handwriting may suffer because you are trying to get too many ideas down too fast. One way of keeping up your speed without scribbling is to work out a set of abbreviations.

For instance, you should have short ways of writing special terms that are common in your particular subject. In Psychology, for example, you might usefully have contractions for words like: experiment, behavior, conditioning, memory, correlation, gestalt, psychology, and so on.

And for common phrases that are needed in practically every subject, you'll probably know most of the fairly standard abbreviations below:

e.g.	i.e.	c.f.	N.B.	$=$	$\neq$	$<$	$>$	$\therefore$	$\because$

Can you match them against these phrases?

1. greater than
2. less than
3. because
4. therefore
5. equals, is the same as
6. compare, remember in this context
7. does not equal, is different from
8. note well, important
9. that is
10. for example

---

1. *greater than* (>)
2. *less than* (<)
3. *because* (∵)
4. *therefore* (∴)
5. *equals, is the same as* (=)
6. *compare, remember in this context* (c.f.)
7. *does not equal, is different from* (≠)
8. *note well, important* (N.B.)
9. *that is* (i.e.)
10. *for example* (e.g.)

7.18 There are only two rules with abbreviations:
1. Make up your system and stick to it. (Don't be inconsistent.)
2. Don't use your abbreviations in material other people will have to read.

Layout. Use every trick of layout you can to make your notes *look memorable*—as an arrangement on the page. The more logical and/or dramatic they look on the page, the more easily you will be able to picture them in your mind's eye. And this will help in examinations.

Which kind of notes are automatically laid out in a logical, almost "pictorial" fashion?
a. summaries, or
b. outlines.

---

b. *outlines*

7.19 To make summary notes as effective as an outline, you'll have to go to a bit more trouble with spacing and layout. (Do *not* try to make them look like paragraphs in a book.)

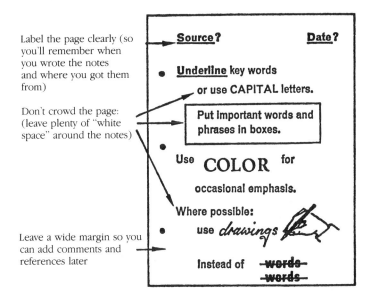

With your page of notes laid out in this fashion, you should be able to close your eyes and bring the notes back to mind as a *picture*. (Try it now with the page shown above.)

How will this *help* you?

You should find it easier to remember the wording of your notes if you can picture the layout. (Well-spaced notes are always easier to recall than a cramped and crowded page.)

TAKING NOTES IN LECTURES

7.20 Despite the practical difficulties of the lecture situation, your *aim* should be to produce easily-read *outlines* of the kind you would make from your reading.

Use SQ3R

The best approach to a lecture is to use the SQ_3R technique, as far as you can. *Surveying* a lecture in advance is something you can't easily do, but you should be alert for any remarks from the lecturer that indicate the ground he or she is to cover.

Questioning, however, may not be so difficult. Presumably you know what was said last time, you may have done some reading, and you perhaps have some expectations about what is to come. Approach the lecture in a critical, questioning state of mind, and keep framing questions (even if you don't need to ask them) throughout.

In lectures, of course, you don't *read*: instead you _____ .

---

listen

7.21   And the *listen* step involves you in a very complex task. Simultaneously, you must hear, analyze, select, and record. Not only must you pick out the lecturer's *main ideas* as he or she speaks, and grasp the *overall structure* of the argument, but also, and *at the same time,* you must string together a set of readable *notes* that will bring it all back to mind.

In what ways can a skillful lecturer help to make this task simpler for you?

He can write his main headings on the chalkboard; he can preview at the beginning of each section and summarize at the end; he can draw your attention to the most vital points. (You may have thought of yet other ways.)

7.22   Admittedly, not all lecturers are equally helpful in this, and your note-taking tactics will have to be flexible enough to cope with quite a variety of individual lecturing styles. Even so, you will sometimes find it extremely difficult to organize your notes as you are writing them, or even to be sure of what the main points are supposed to be.

Some students deal with this by taking copious notes and hoping to see some pattern emerge from them by the time the lecture ends. Others struggle to grasp the lecturer's line of argument, taking very few notes even if it means missing out some of the main points.

Do you tend to take a great many notes in lectures, or very few? Why?

Possibly, your practice will vary from one lecture to another. (It might pay you to try and account for the differences.)

7.23 On the whole, it is perhaps better to err on the side of too *few* notes rather than too many, *provided*:
   1. This better enables you to grasp the essentials of the lecturer's argument.
   2. You are prepared to write up a full set of notes soon after the lecture is over.
   But this brings us to the next, *vitally important,* step in applying SQ₃R to the lecture situation:

Having done your best to *survey, question,* and *listen* to the lecture, you must now try to _____ what was said.

---

recall

7.24 Never be content with your notes as they stand at the end of a lecture. By comparison with reading-notes they are almost certain to be *incomplete* and somewhat *disorganized.* Go away and rethink them. With your notes in front of you, try to *reconstruct* the lecture in your memory.
   This first attempt at recall is something many students shy away from, yet it can dramatically halt the process of forgetting. (*Without* an attempt at recall, most students forget 75 percent of what they have heard in a lecture within one week—and in less than three weeks they have forgotten 98 percent of it.)

How soon after the lecture should you first force yourself to recall what you have heard?
   a. Immediately after, or
   b. One week later, or
   c. More than one week later.

---

a. *Immediately after. (Even then you may remember only 50 percent of what was said.)*

7.25 While the lecture is still fresh in your mind you can think it through again, correcting your misunderstandings, adding detail to your notes, and giving them more shape. Discipline yourself to do this *within a few hours* of every lecture and you'll reap huge benefits; leave it too long and you may find your lecture notes simply don't make sense.

In the course of trying to *recall,* you may often wish you could take the final step of the SQ$_3$R method: That is, you wish you could _____ what was actually said.

---

review

7.26 Unfortunately, you can't review (or re-hear) the actual words spoken (unless the lecture was tape recorded). But what you can do, if you sense a worrying gap in your notes, is go and ask the lecturer about it. Normally, he or she will be happy to review any point that has eluded you.

Who else can you check with, besides the lecturer?

You can check with fellow-students *who attended the lecture with you. Did they get points, or see some theme or structure of ideas, that you missed?*

7.27 If you and some of your fellow-students are agreed on the need to improve note-taking, you might sit down and check each other's notes after each lecture (and maybe after a piece of reading you've all done also).

A Check List

Perhaps your group could agree on a check list of faults that your notes should avoid. Here is one such list:

1. *General Format*
   a. Notebook too small/big
   b. Pages too crowded/spread out
   c. Handwriting illegible
   d. Topics mixed together
2. *Structure of Notes*
   a. Poor labeling at top
   b. Not in outline form (too much solid prose)

    c. Insufficient use of headings, numbers, indents, emphasis
    d. Hard to see organization and relationships of ideas
3. *Content and Phrasing*
    a. Missed some of main ideas
    b. Too much detail
    c. Too wordy
    d. Wording unclear
    e. Too much in author's words, not own
    f. Missed, or misdrew, important graphs, tables, etc.

Once a checklist was agreed upon, each set of notes could be assessed by each student in the group, and all should learn from the ensuing discussion.

N.B. Don't forget to *RECALL* and *REVIEW* this chapter before going further.

Then tackle the review questions.

REVIEW QUESTIONS

7.28 What are the *two* main benefits to be had from writing notes? (Frames 1–2)

Note-taking keeps you actively concentrating, and provides a written record from which you can revise.

7.29 What is the advantage of using a *loose-leaf* binder for your notes? (Frame 3)

You are not tied down by the order in which you wrote your notes: you can rearrange them under topics as you wish, rewrite individual pages, and add to them at any point.

7.30 At what stage of SQ$_3$R is it best to make notes? (Frames 5–6)

    a. At the *read* step, or
    b. Between *read* and *recall,* or
    c. At the *recall* step.

---

    c. *At the* recall *step. (At the read step you would be too close to the author's words, and there is no step between read and recall.)*

7.31 If you haven't done so already, make an *outline* of the chapter (7) you have just read. (Frames 7–15)

How does your outline compare with this one?

 I. The *value* of notes is that they:
  A. Keep you active and concentrating.
  B. Provide a written record for revision.
 II. Store notes in a loose-leaf binder (for flexibility).
 III. *Writing* the notes:
  A. Contents should include:
   1. Author's main ideas and important detail.
   2. Logical plan of his argument (essentials only).
  B. Make notes at *recall* step.
  C. Use your own words.
  D. Use *outline* form (rather than summary) where possible:
   1. Expand headings and re-state topic sentences.
   2. Put important detail in brackets.
   3. Use indentation, and ⎫
   4. ... letters and numbers ⎬ to show relationships.
  E. *Mechanics:*
   1. Write clearly or type.
   2. Work out set of abbreviations.
   3. Use logical/dramatic layout on page:
    a. New page for each set of notes—label clearly.
    b. Plenty of "white space," and wide margins.
    c. Color, diagrams, emphasize key points, etc.
 IV. In *lectures:*
  A. Try to use SQ$_3$R
  B. Write few notes rather than many, if:
   1. This enables you to follow the lecturer's argument.
   2. You write up fuller notes soon after lecture.
  C. Check and revise your notes within a few hours of the lecture:
   1. Reconstruct the lecture in your mind (recall).
   2. Correct your notes, add detail, give them shape.
  D. Review lecture by discussion with:
   1. Teachers.
   2. Fellow-students. (Compare notes against group check list?)

7.32 Do you believe a page of summary notes should be densely packed with the vital information or that it should carry fewer ideas, more widely spaced? Why?
(Frames 18–20)

Well-spaced notes are usually preferable, even though they use up more paper. The less you put on one page, the more easily you can picture it and bring it back to mind.

7.33 In applying SQ₃R to a lecture, what would you do at the *recall* step? *When* would you do it? (Frames 24–25)

As soon as possible *after the lecture, you would try to reconstruct the lecture in your mind, correct your notes, add detail, and put them into a more organized shape.*

7.34 How might you "review" the lecture to check the accuracy of your recall? (Frames 26–27)

You could check with friends who also heard the lecture, or even with the lecturer himself.

7.35 Now we come to the final chapter—How to Deal with Examinations. Like chapters 4 and 6, this chapter also is in continuous (unprogrammed) prose: but it has far fewer headings or "visual signposts" to help the reader. Thus (while still "a cinch" compared with many textbooks) it gives you a rather more demanding test of your ability to sort out main ideas and the way they are organized.
    So, when you are ready to go on:

1. Study chapter 8, using all five steps of the SQ₃R approach. (You will probably need to recall at least twice *before* you reach the end of the chapter.)
2. Write a well-organized set of *outline* notes.

8 How to Deal with Examinations
(**Study Time: about 40 minutes**)

Whatever we may think of them, examinations are part of our way of life. A student hardly needs to be told this. He realizes that examinations are going to help determine his future. Regular (at mid-term, the end of each semester, or yearly) examinations still decide whether, or under what conditions, he is allowed to continue in school; a final examination will decide whether or not he gets the qualification awarded to those who have successfully completed the course.

Since not only personal self-esteem but also career prospects may dwindle drastically if the final degree is not obtained, there is little wonder that many students approach examinations with some anxiety. Unfortunately, this can get out of hand. While a certain amount of mild tension is unavoidable (and may indeed be psychologically valuable) some students take refuge in "exam anxiety" as an escape from the unconscious guilt they feel at having wasted the time that leads up to the examination: by "going to pieces" they hope to attract sympathy instead of blame. (No one who has worked through this program so far could possibly fall into this category!)

Basically, the situation is this: Examinations are put together and graded in such a way that the student who has satisfied the entry requirements for his particular course can perform reasonably well in the exam—*provided* he has applied his intelligence to the course and has prepared properly. If he fails to do himself justice in the examination it will probably be because of faults either in his *preparation,* or in his examination *techniques.*

So what can the student do to ensure that he is properly prepared? How can he perform to the best of his ability on the day of the examination? These are the questions we'll try to answer in this final chapter.

PREPARING FOR EXAMINATIONS

The surest way to examination success is to conscientiously apply effective study techniques over a period of time. If you even approximately follow the advice we've worked out in this book (scheduling your study, SQ$_3$R, systematic note-taking, etc.) your chances will be enormously improved. You will remember more, have a better understanding, and be able to organize your ideas quickly and effectively. Such skills are rewarded in examinations as they are in other areas of human activity.

Of course, the key role in preparing for tests and examinations is played by *revision.* Literally, this means "to see again." Few of us can grasp an idea in all its possible aspects and applications simply from one exposure to it. We need to "see it again," often many times and preferably from many different angles, before it really becomes part of our understanding.

When should you start revising for an examination? The answer is *now.* To get results, revision must be a regular part of your study routine, right from the beginning of the course. All the time, as you meet new ideas, you should be looking back over the ideas you have already met, testing and refreshing your memory about them, and "seeing them again" in the light of your more recent experience.

There are two very good reasons for doing regular revision right from the start. For one thing, you simply wouldn't have the time (or peace of mind) to revise everything in the course if you left it all to the last minute. Second, and more important, early revisions will make later material *easier to learn* since you will already have a firm understanding of what precedes it: the more you have learned, the easier it is to learn more.

As the examination draws near, of course, you will need to be quite systematic about your revision. For the final five or six weeks you should work out a revision *schedule*. Make a list of the topics that have to be revised, and decide in what order they should be tackled. Space out the revision for each topic and make a note of what you intend to revise during each day of your revision schedule. To keep up interest it is usually better to revise a *variety* of topics each day rather than devote yourself to one topic exclusively. Don't forget to leave plenty of time for rest and recreation, *especially* in the last few days before the examination.

So revision must start early in your courses as a regular part of the routine of study. As examinations approach it must be scheduled very seriously, so that you don't find you've left everything to the last week. All right, we know *when* to revise: the next question is *how*?

One very valuable way to revise is to join up with a couple of fellow-students who are taking the same course as you, and meet together two or three times a week to revise topics as a *group*. Clearly, you have to make sure you can all get along, and it does demand a certain maturity of outlook and self-discipline to ensure that such revision sessions remain purposeful and do not degenerate into trivial chit-chat. But the benefits of working as a member of a group rather than on your own are great enough to make the effort worthwhile.

For one thing, it helps you be much more objective about the course. Working by yourself you can be so attracted by one area of the syllabus that you completely overlook some other equally vital areas. Within a group, however, other people's preferences are likely to differ from yours, and you can help make each other aware of the syllabus as a whole, and thus the possible coverage of the examination paper.

Also, on account of this difference of interests, each member of the group is likely to find herself "teaching" the others whenever her special topics come under discussion. And, as all teachers know, the best way to learn something yourself is to teach it to somebody else.

Psychologically also, it is valuable to work as a member of a revision group, rather than in solitary confinement. The human contact can help you keep a sense of proportion about the impending event, and thereby lessens the anxiety that might otherwise build up.

In order to revise for an examination it should be obvious that you must find out all you can about that examination. Get hold of a copy of the syllabus: What topics are prescribed? Look at past examination sheets: What sort of questions are asked? Are questions on some topics compulsory? How long do you get to answer each question?

The reason I suggest finding out all you can about the syllabus and the examination is that, during your revision, you should *practice doing what the examination will require you to do.*

For instance, the examination will aim to measure what you can *recall* from your studying. So, in revising, you should put the emphasis on recall rather than on rereading. As I've mentioned before, the fact that you can recognize ideas when you read them again is no guarantee that you'd recall them in an examination. Therefore, when you come to read your notes again and perhaps check the textbooks, you should only do so *after* having tried to recall the main ideas they contain.

Furthermore, it is unlikely that the examination paper will require you to display your facts and ideas in the same form they were in when you first came across them. In the examination you will be called upon to *recombine* your ideas and use them in *new ways.* Try to reorganize your knowledge, form new associations of ideas, and look at things from many points of view. Apart from being a more appropriate training for the examination, this approach is also more interesting than if you were drearily to retrace your original learning path.

Revising as a member of a group is a very good way of learning to look at a topic in a new light. In a group of three or four students there are usually several opinions, and a topic does seem to take on a new significance once it has been the subject of a heated debate.

It is also helpful in reorganizing your learning if you revise all your material on a particular topic at once. Take all your notes (whether from textbooks, tapes, films, lectures, or seminars) along with your essays or papers and old examination answers, and work on them all together. Viewed again in this way, you may see associations of ideas that were not evident before, and you may clear up earlier misunderstandings.

Similarly, it can be illuminating to revise two or three *related* topics at the same time. Although you first studied them separately you may now find many common strands linking the topics together. Thus you get to see each topic in a new light and you have an extra set of associations to help jog your memory.

In trying to get new viewpoints, *force* yourself to view differently. In working through your old notes and essays, be critical. This shouldn't be too difficult. After all, you are now older (whether by weeks, months, or years) than you were when you wrote them. Do they now seem at all unclear, ignorant, muddled, misguided, cocksure, one-sided, embarrassing? Try to uncover their weaknesses. Track down your omissions and faults of emphasis. Assault your notes and essays with the newer ideas and more mature viewpoints you will have acquired since you first wrote them. Use them as an opportunity to test out your newer understandings.

Then rewrite your notes ruthlessly. Write summaries and condensed outlines that contain the essential ideas of all your original notes and essays on a topic but which are much shorter and which you've updated in the light of more recent experience.

So it is advisable to emphasize *recall* and *reorganization* of knowledge in your revision, because these will be the general activities required of you in the examination. But it is wise to practice also the more specific skill required of you: that is, the *answering of examination questions.*

For most examinations the question sheets from previous years are available. Get a set of them and analyze the questions that have been asked over the last few years. Collect questions together according to topic. Then try to answer them.

Don't just browse through the papers telling yourself "Yes, I could manage numbers 1, 4, and 7, but I'd be in trouble with 2, 3, and 6." You can't really be sure of how you'd do until you actually practice answering such questions.

One of the most useful ways of giving yourself practice is simply to write answers in *outline* form. Weigh the question, decide what it is asking for, then jot down the main ideas and important detail that you would want to bring into your answer. Then write down the key steps of your argument as a skeleton outline, just as you would before writing a normal essay.

A similar approach can be used in a revision group. Each member can show or speak his outline to the rest of the group and have his argument discussed. Clearly it can be valuable for all members to answer the same question, for comparison of the different answers may be instructive for everyone. Another variation is for the group to take half a dozen questions on a common topic, revise around that topic, and allocate a question at random for each member of the group to answer. And, of course, members can also make up their own questions for fellow-students to answer.

Since planning is the most crucial step in answering a question, you will be pretty safe in spending most of your practice time in writing plans for answers. (Especially since you can plan two or three answers in the time it would take you to plan and write out the complete answer for just one question.)

However, at least now and again, you would be wise to write out complete *model answers*. Time yourself, though. Work out how long you would be allowed in the examination room and then both plan and write your essay within that time. Some students even find it helpful to spend one morning a week for the last two or three weeks actually putting themselves through a mock examination. That is, they sit down with an unfamiliar paper and, under examination conditions, spend three hours or whatever is allowed in coming up with the best answers they can manage. If you have any doubts about your ability to concentrate and work flat out for the period of the examination, this is an excellent way of breaking yourself in—so at least you won't expire from shock on the day. Again, these dummy runs can be even more useful if done within your revision group and followed up by comparison of answers and discussion.

Keep all your practice answers, whether outline notes or full essays. They will be particularly valuable for last-minute revision of vital topics.

One warning. In the course of your revision you may find yourself predicting that certain questions are "bound" to come up in your exam. Have bets with yourself by all means, but don't pin too much reliance on being right. Certainly don't neglect other areas of the syllabus: don't over-specialize.

Students have been trying to out-guess examiners for years and they never succeed: the examiners have always been at it longer than any student.

To sum up, successful revision needs to be started early: it demands that you find out all you can about the examination and that you practice doing the things you will have to do in the examination room (that is, giving out ideas, rather than taking them in); and it is often most useful if done as a member of a revision group.

All too soon perhaps, your revision schedule has been eaten away and you reach the last day before the examination. Students spend this day in a variety of ways, according to temperament. Some believe in switching off all conscious thought of the exam and doing no work at all. For others it is so difficult to keep their minds off the exam that they find it less of a strain simply to continue normal revision. If you are one who must keep at it, make absolutely sure it *is* revision you are doing, and not new learning. Trying to learn new things at this stage would only block out things you've learned previously.

One thing you can profitably do the evening before the examination is to make sure you have all the items of equipment you'll need next day: a watch, a couple of pens (with ink), pencils, ruler, mathematical instruments, and whatever else is likely to be useful in the examination room.

If you do spend the last day revising, make sure you break off at least two hours before bedtime (or you'll be carrying on relentlessly in your sleep). Read something entertaining, watch television, or chat with any of your friends who are not obsessed by examinations. Go to bed early and get a good night's sleep. Remember that next morning a fresh, alert mind will be far more useful to you than a few extra facts packed in behind a sickening headache.

THE DAY OF THE EXAMINATION

Some wit has pointed out that most students take each examination three times: on the way to the examination room, again when they get there, and a third time going home. And unfortunately they only get credit for one of these performances.

If you can, avoid doing a "preview" on the way to the examination. Especially avoid talking about the prospects with other candidates: you'll only get depressed and dispirited at the thought of all the topics you should have paid attention to and haven't. Keep to yourself, and remain confident that you've done everything humanly possible (because if you haven't it's now too late to worry). If you must think about the forthcoming test, let your thoughts be specific: concentrate on just one possible question and organize an outline answer in your mind.

So, at last, the moment arrives. You are mildly tense, keyed-up to respond to the challenge, but you are certainly not in fear and trembling. You are *prepared*.

Once you have the examination sheet in your hand, read it *right through* very carefully. Too many students hunt frantically for the first question that looks vaguely familiar, let out a gasp of relief, and plunge straight into an answer without so much as a glance at the other questions or the instructions to candidates.

Spend at least the first five minutes of your time just reading through and getting the "feel" of the test. Look first at the instructions to candidates. How long have you got? How many questions do you have to answer? Do any of them carry more points than others? Are any of them compulsory? Is the test divided into two or more sections, with so many questions to be answered from each? Does each answer have to be started on a new sheet of paper? And so on.

You'll probably know most of these answers from your practice with previous tests, but it pays to check, for the rules may have been changed. Every examination brings its rueful crop of students who've spoiled their chances by answering four questions instead of three (or vice versa), or who didn't realize they had to answer *all* the questions in Section A, or who thought they had three hours (not two) for the test, and so on.

Then pay individual attention to each and every question. Make sure that you know what each question is asking for (even if you can't provide the answer), and also what it is *not* asking for. Be objective, and don't misread the questions. Don't try (as many students do) to twist them into the questions you *wish* had been asked.

You must also be sure of *precisely* what the question requires you to *do*. Look for the key *verb* that tells you what kind of answer to give. Here is a list of the ones most commonly used in examination questions:

Analyze	Illustrate
Assess	Interpret
Comment	Justify
Compare	List
Contrast	Outline
Criticize	Prove
Define	Reconcile
Describe	Relate
Discuss	Review
Enumerate	State
Evaluate	Summarize
Explain	Trace

Needless to say, if you "describe" when you are asked to "analyze" or if you "define" instead of "enumerating" you have failed to answer the question. And you'll get no credit if you simply "write around" the subject. If you are in any doubt about the differences in meaning among these twenty-odd verbs, you'd be wise to go to a good dictionary and compile your own glossary of "examinese."

After you have considered every question on the test, and perhaps put a pencil mark next to those that seem "possibles," you should be ready to make your final choice. Be very wise in this. Avoid if you can the "easy" question that everybody can answer: the examiner will soon tire of wading through the hack responses and he or she won't thank you for adding to them. Look for questions that will allow you to show your own personal flair. But, at the same time, don't get out of your depth by taking on a question that's too tough for you: there is no extra credit for bravery.

The next step (yes, you may not have written a word yet), is to *budget your time.* How long can you spend on each question? The best plan is to allocate your time according to the number of points given for each question. If all carry equal weight then you divide your time up equally. So you have perhaps four questions to answer in three hours. How long per question? Not three-quarters of an hour, for you'll have used up five or ten minutes by the time you come to start planning your first answer, and you should allow yourself another ten or fifteen minutes spare at the end for a final check on all answers. So, you may decide you have forty minutes or less to spend on each question. Look at the clock and write down the *actual times* by which you expect to have finished each question.

You are now ready to plan out your answers. Before you begin writing you should have a *skeleton outline* of the kind we have discussed before: more than ever, in the time-limited examination situation, you need this as a firm guide to your writing. Furthermore, even if you decide not to submit the outline on your answer paper, the examiner will be impressed with its results, for your answer will be a logical, well-organized argument rather than a rag-bag of jumbled outpourings. (Besides, students who have run out of time in an examination often get almost as many points for submitting a clear outline as they would have been awarded for a complete essay.)

With each question, then, jot down the main ideas and important details that occur to you. Do a bit of free association and just let the ideas come to mind as they will. Not all will be equally useful, but make a note of them regardless. Then sort them out, and write an outline of your argument in the usual way. At least a quarter of your total answer time should be spent planning and outlining.

Some students would recommend that you outline *every* answer before writing out any one of them in full. There are three benefits to be had from this approach: First, you can more easily treat your answers as a set, and avoid the possibility of repeating yourself from one to another. Second, you are giving your unconscious mind a chance to work for you: having planned out all the answers, your unconscious is likely to carry on the train of thought even while you are writing the first answers, and so may come up with fresh associations that will help you in writing the later ones. Third, once the preliminary planning is complete, you have the comfort of knowing exactly what ground you've got to cover in the remainder of the time, and all you have left to do is expand on your outlines. It takes nerve to spend perhaps the first hour in writing the complete set of detailed outlines, but the results can be very rewarding.

Once you start writing your answers, success or failure

depends on your *sense of priorities*. Begin by answering your best question (or the compulsory question if there is one). Keep your mind on one question at a time but be prepared to jot down any ideas that may suddenly occur to you for use in other answers.

Watch the clock and stick firmly to the time-limits you set yourself. If you run out of time on a particular answer (or if you get bogged down on it), *stop writing*. Leave a big space on your answer sheet in case you can come back to finish off later, but get right on with the next question. In the peculiar arithmetic of examinations, ½ + ½ is usually greater than 1, and two half-answered questions will normally earn you more points than one complete answer. Many students fail because they spend too long on their "best" questions.

In your writing, concentrate on saying what is most worth saying: if you are running short of time, get the main ideas down and don't worry too much about the detail. Be concise: very often 50 percent could be cut from a student's answer without losing him any points.

The style of your written answers should be the same as that of other essays you write—simple, direct, and to the point. Pay attention to spelling and grammar: be particularly careful not to misspell words that appear on the question paper. But, above all, *write legibly*. Your answer sheets have to be read and marked by human beings, not machines; and if they find difficulty reading your words they are likely to be less sympathetic toward your ideas.

Don't rush away from the examination room the moment you've written your last word. Save yourself a few minutes at the end to give all your answers a final check: you should search for slips of the pen (a vital "not" left out of a sentence), for miscalculations (in numerical examples), for clumsy expressions, for faulty spelling or grammar, and for illegible phrases that can be rewritten. Such a final check is never a waste of time: it is simply a professional way to finish off the job, and many a student picks up 5 to 10 percent of his final grade in this last going-over. Besides, it is better to have a last-minute inspiration while checking through your test than on the way home.

But, when it really is all over, don't hang around for those depressing postmortems with other students. They rarely make you joyful about the answers you have written, and too often they leave you brooding about all the things you've left unsaid. This can be very unsettling if you have another examination looming ahead; so it's best to get away, enjoy some rest and recreation, and then resume training for your next exam.

LEARNING FROM EXAMINATIONS

In conclusion, it's worth remembering that most examinations are *not* end-of-course examinations, and it is possible to *learn* from your performance in them. The typical student pays very little attention to her answer sheet if it is returned to her (other than to moan about the grade and check whether the teacher has added any amusing comments); but very often it could teach her a lot about how to prepare for the next exam.

If you have your paper returned, analyze each answer against the original question, and consider the examiner's comments and grading. If possible, compare your answer with those of other students, and ask your professor for comment. Where did you lose credit? Did you misinterpret the question? Did you leave out some important ideas or some vital supporting detail? Was your answer badly planned or illogical? Did you misunderstand some vital part of the course? Or did your memory let you down? How would you write the answer if this question were to come up again? How can you avoid having the same trouble with another question in a later examination? By analyzing your mistakes in this way you can uncover faults in your study technique and remedy them before it is too late.

8.1 Now:

1. *Recall* the final section, and the chapter as a whole.
2. Finish off your *outline* notes.
3. *Review* the whole chapter to check and neaten up your outline.

Then, before you compare your outline with that drawn up by another reader, work through the following review questions. (They may remind you of something your outline has overlooked.)

REVIEW QUESTIONS

8.2 Suppose you have to take an examination one year from now: about when should you *begin* to revise for it? (Page 119)

Begin now.

8.3 Which of the following activities should you stress most in your revision: reading; recalling; reviewing? Why? (Page 121)

The emphasis should be on recalling, *because this is what you will be required to do in the examination itself.*

8.4 The examination will also require you to recombine your ideas and use them in new ways. Describe at least two ways of preparing yourself for this. (Pages 121–122)

You can discuss topics with other students; you can revise all your notes from all sources (on a given topic) at once; you can revise two related topics at the same time; you can be ruthless in criticizing and rewriting your old notes.

8.5 What is the third thing—a specific skill—that a written examination will require of you? How can you prepare yourself? (Page 122)

The writing of essays. You can prepare yourself by working with past papers: plan outline answers, write complete model answers, take mock exams.

8.6 What are all the preliminary jobs you must do between being handed the examination and beginning to write out an answer to your first question? (Pages 125–127)

Read through the exam sheet (checking instructions, weighing questions, and deciding which ones to answer); budget your time; write outline plans for at least one of your answers.

8.7 If you were pressed for time, would you prefer to hand in one answer completely written out in detail, or two answers outlined in skeleton form? Why? (Pages 127–128)

Two well-planned outlines would be likely to get you a better grade than one answer written out in full.

8.8 What would you do if you finished writing your last answer and found you still had ten minutes left before the end of the examination? (Page 128)

Presumably you would use the time to check through all your answers and add the finishing touches that might well add appreciably to your overall grade.

8.9 And now:
CHECK your outline against the following one, which was written by one of the students who helped me test this program by reading it through before publication. Did you pick out the same "hierarchy of ideas" as he did? Did you include more or less detail? Have you noted anything vital that he has missed, or vice versa?

from *Learn How to Study* (ch. 8) by D. Rowntree 14/12/83

How to Deal with Examinations (Good preparation + exam technique).

    I. Examination success demands *preparation:*
        A. Apply effective study techniques over period of time.
        B. Revise systematically:
            1. Start *now;* because
                a. Never enough time later.
                b. Future work will come more easily.
            2. Make a *schedule* for revision.
                a. Space out revision for each topic.
                b. Tackle variety of topics each day.
                c. Allow plenty rest and recreation.
            3. Form a revision *group* (3 friends, 3 times a week).
                a. Fosters objectivity.

        b. Learn by teaching others.

        c. Keeps you sane.

    4. Practice doing what the exam *requires* of you:

        a. Emphasis on recall (not recognition).

        b. Reorganize your ideas by:

           i. Discussing with others.

          ii. Revising *all* notes on a topic at once.

         iii. Revising related topics together.

         iv. Criticizing own notes.

          v. Rewriting notes.

        c. Tackle old examination questions:

           i. Write outline plans for answers.

          ii. Write complete model answers.

         iii. Take mock exams.

         iv. Don't try to out-guess examiner.

  C. On the *day before* the exam:

    1. Do not learn *new* things.

    2. Revise normally or relax completely.

    3. Gather exam equipment.

    4. Go to bed early.

II. *Technique* on the day of the examination:

  A. Don't discuss prospects with other students.

  B. Read right through exam sheet (5 min.):

    1. What instructions to candidates?

    2. Decide what each question is asking for (key verbs).

    3. Choose your best questions.

  C. *Budget* your time:

    1. Allocate total time according to points per question.

    2. Leave 10–15 minutes at end for checking.

    3. Note expected finishing time for each question.

  D. Plan your answers:

    1. Jot down main ideas and important details.

    2. Form them into a skeleton outline.

    3. Outline *all* answers before writing any up ($\frac{1}{4}$ + of all answer time).

  E. Keep a sense of *priorities:*

    1. Answer best question first.

    2. Stick to your time-budget ($\frac{1}{2} + \frac{1}{2} > 1!$).

    3. Concentrate on main issues.

  F. Write:

    1. Simply, directly, and to the point.

        2. Grammatically, and without misspelling.

        3. Legibly.

    G. When finished writing:

        1. Check through all answers ('till time is up).

        2. Don't stay for postmortem discussions.

III. *Learn* from examinations by:

    A. Checking examiner's marks and comments against questions.

    B. Comparing your answers with other students'.

    C. Discussing your performance with teacher.

    D. Remedying any faults revealed in study techniques.

Finally:

Please remember that my purpose in this book has not been to teach you how to study but to persuade you to teach yourself. At the very least, I hope I have convinced you that study is a job with its own professional work skills; and I believe we have worked out a way of talking about this job that will enable you to examine future study problems objectively and discuss them fruitfully with teachers and fellow-students. All that's left now is for me to wish you GOOD LUCK in all your studies and examinations.

Bibliography

(In case you might wish to give yourself a refresher course from time to time!)

Armstrong, W. H. (1967). *Study is Hard Work,* 2nd ed. (New York: Harper & Row).

Emmet, E. R. (1965). *Learning to Think* (London: Longman; New York: Philosophical Library).

*Hill, W. F. (1977). *Learning Thru Discussion* (Beverly Hills, Calif.: Sage).

*James, D. E. (1967). *A Student's Guide to Efficient Study* (London: Pergamon).

*Leedy, P. D. (1963). *Read With Speed and Precision* (New York: McGraw-Hill).

Lindgren, H. C. (1969). *The Psychology of College Success* (London: Wiley; Melbourne, Fla.: Krieger, 1980).

Maddox, H. (1978). *How to Study* (New York: Fawcett).

*Morgan, C. T., et al. (1979). *How to Study,* 3rd ed. (New York: McGraw-Hill).

Parsons, C. J. (1973). *Theses & Project Work* (London: Allen & Unwin).

Robinson, F. P. (1970). *Effective Study,* 4th ed. (New York: Harper & Row).

*particularly recommended

Index

Index

The entries in this index refer mainly to frame numbers. However, the entries for chapters 4, 6, and 8—where there is continuous prose without frame numbers—are identified by page numbers.